DID YOU KNOW THAT . . .

- Carol Burnett grew up coping with parents who loved her—but loved drinking more?

- her start in New York was an interest-free loan with a pass-it-on provision for others?

- her first TV appearance held a secret greeting for her grandmother—a tug on the ear that meant "hello"?

- she turned down Streisand's "Funny Girl" role?

- that her first daughter was on TV before she was two years old?

- that Carol's First-Lady imitations made Lady Bird happy and Pat huffy?

These are just a few of the personal insights *THE CAROL BURNETT STORY* reveals about the girl who looks like almost anybody and performs like no one else in the world.

Books by George Carpozi, Jr.

The Carol Burnett Story
The Brigitte Bardot Story
Vince Edwards
The Hidden Side of Jacqueline Kennedy
The Gary Cooper Story
The Johnny Cash Story
The John Wayne Story
The Bobby Sherman Story

THE
CAROL
BURNETT
STORY

by George Carpozi, Jr.

**WARNER
PAPERBACK
LIBRARY**

A Warner Communications Company

WARNER PAPERBACK LIBRARY EDITION
First Printing: July, 1975

Cover design by Lynn Kaplan

Cover photograph by Henry Grossman © TIME/LIFE Syndication

Photograph section designed by Milton Batalion

Warner Paperback Library is a division of Warner Books, Inc.,
75 Rockefeller Plaza, New York, N.Y. 10019.

 A Warner Communications Company

Printed in the United States of America

Not associated with Warner Press, Inc. of Anderson, Indiana

THE
CAROL BURNETT
STORY

1

Red-haired, green-eyed Carol Burnett was born April 26, 1933, in San Antonio, Texas, and the early handicaps she faced illustrate how adversity can be overcome.

Her mother and father were alcoholics.

Miss Burnett does not try to hide this about her parents.

"I have thought a great deal about it and I feel I'd rather have it come from me than some outside source that would be cruel or misleading about it," says Carol. "I didn't want to read anything like, 'I knew her when her father was a drunk. . . .'"

The family did not live long in San Antonio. Carol was only eight years old in 1941 when her mother and father moved to California to seek better opportunities. But Hollywood, where the family settled, proved no success. Carol remembers:

"Our economic circumstances, you could say, were stringent. In fact, we were downright poor. And, of course, we were on welfare a good deal of the time."

Carol was born in the early days of the Great Depression. Her father, Jody, was earning a respectable living as manager of a movie theater in San Antonio. He had moved there from Arkansas with his family years earlier. Carol almost made her natal debut in the loge of that flick. Her mother, Louise, who always got in free of course, was watching a matinee performance of *Rasputin and the Empress*, starring the three Barrymores—John, Ethel, and Lionel.

"The time suddenly came and my mother knew she couldn't wait to see the end of the picture," Carol said. "But Mom seldom missed the finale or, for that matter, any portion of any picture showing at the movie house my father managed, after I was born. The movie theater was my environment, too. Mom took me there every day. Then later on when I grew old enough, I'd go there on my own. I darn near lived at the movies, in the shadow of the silver screen."

It was different in Hollywood. By then Carol's father, always a heavy drinker, was hitting the bottle without let-up.

"Although my dad drank ever since I could remember," Carol said, "my mother didn't. But then she started drinking to keep him company. So she became an alcoholic."

Bickering and fights during their alcoholic stupors led to misunderstandings and disenchantment in their rare sober moments. Eventually Jody moved out, leaving his wife with little Carol. But in her condition Mrs. Burnett was not always up to taking care of the child. So her mother, Mrs. Mae White, took granddaughter Carol to live with her and quickly became the stabilizing influence in the little girl's chaotic life.

"Sure it was a tough childhood," Carol admitted, "but not any tougher than any other kids on the block. I was loved. My parents had their problems, but they loved me. A lot of kids whose parents don't drink and who have money don't have that—the love of their mother and father."

Carol's grandmother lived in a room and a half in a low-rent apartment house at Wilcox and Yucca Street that was furnished with two Murphy beds and not much else.

"I slept in one of the couches and my closet was the bathroom shower rack because Grandma was a pack rat," recalled Carol. "Everything was in her closet. So I'd hang my clothes on the shower rack. And consequently nobody could ever take a shower. We took baths, of course. But to get into the tub we'd have to push my clothes aside. Those duds, you could say, were always well steamed."

A little later on when Carol was in her teens and boys wanted to meet her, she'd never let them near the house.

"My grandmother was a very messy housekeeper and I was embarrassed," Carol remembers. "So we'd sit in the lobby of a hotel and talk, but never in the house. I never brought anybody there if I could help it."

Now and then some boy or girl would drop in unexpectedly, and she did her utmost to usher the visitor out as quickly as she could. Once or twice the uninvited guests asked to use the cluttered bathroom.

"But they never did," Carol said with a shrug. "If they had to go, I'd always tell them it was out of order and send them to the Shell station across the street."

Living with her grandmother didn't impose a great geographic separation upon Carol and her parents. For much of the time that Carol lived with her grandmother, her mother occupied a flat across the hall in the same apartment building.

"Dad would visit Mom on weekends," Carol remembers, "and that's when I would see him too."

For Mr. and Mrs. Burnett there were also periods of reconciliation. Indeed, during one of those reunions, in 1945, Carol's sister, Antonia Christine, was born. But the Burnett's conjugal compatability did not continue for long. Jody Burnett, drinking harder than ever, left his wife and baby. Yet Carol's memory of her parents, even after all this, holds no bitterness or resentment.

"I never felt unloved," Carol admits. "I remember the wonderful things my parents did for me when they were able to."

One of her fondest recollections of her mother is the time when Carol was on her back with measles. She was unable to sleep—a condition that would later become a chronic problem to be remedied only when she turned to Yoga. But on that particular night her mother wondered whether some other means might not help Carol into slumber.

"Mom asked me whether I thought my favorite drink, Ovaltine, might put me to sleep," Carol said. "I told her I would much rather have chocolate cream pie. So Mother went back to her apartment and baked one—at four o'clock in the morning!"

One of the most heartening acts her father performed for Carol was going on the wagon for almost a year. That happened after Mrs. White had taken ill and was unable to work and make ends meet for Carol's keep.

"It was terrific to see Dad completely sober," Carol admits. "Not that it was so horrendous to see him drunk, because he was a kind drunk. It was my mother who was the nasty drunk. But that happened only when somebody crossed her. She had a very quick tongue and she'd let you have it. Other than that, she was very funny. She had a great sense of humor. She'd sit and drink and play the ukelele in the kitchen and sing songs."

No matter how difficult things were at home, Carol always found refuge in her favorite pastime—the movies. She gets a bit annoyed with herself because her first childhood memory of a movie only goes back to 1937.

"That was in San Antonio when I was four years old," Carol recalls. "I remember seeing Barbara Stanwyck and Joel McCrea. But, darn it, I can't remember any movie before that."

Carol always scrounged the eleven-cents admission for the movies she saw in Hollywood by scavenging milk and soda deposit bottles in her neighborhood. She became highly proficient in this enterprise and consistently managed to raise enough funds for the movies—as often as five times a week. It was that moviegoing habit developed at an early age which ultimately aroused Carol's interest in acting.

"We'd come home and act out the parts," Carol says, laughing at the roles consigned to her. "I almost always ended up playing the male parts because I was a tall, stringy, homely child."

10

Her usual companion on those treks to the theater was a pretty cousin named Janice Vance, who now works as Carol's secretary. Their favorite movies were the Jeanette MacDonald-Nelson Eddy series. Janice always played the blonde soprano while Carol took the baritone's role.

Carol had to wait until she was thirty years old before fulfilling what for her had become a lifelong ambition—playing Jeanette MacDonald. That was in a comedy skit on the *Garry Moore Show* when Carol got her Mountie with a racking Indian love call. What made it all the more satisfying for her was that she was surrounded by twenty Canadian Mounties—each of them the spitting image of Nelson Eddy.

While going to the movies was her obsession, Carol never neglected her schooling. "Thanks to my grandmother, I had a home," says Miss Burnett. "While it wasn't exactly suited for very much serious studying, it nevertheless gave me enough privacy and tranquility to keep me from getting discouraged with my schoolwork."

Her grandmother was a rigid Christian Scientist but she didn't impose her religion on her granddaughter. "Granny was the kind of Christian Scientist who kept aspirin in the cupboard," Carol explains. But she also admits that, as informal as her religious upbringing was, it has made a deep impact on her life.

"I often use Science in my work," Carol admits. "One of the wonderful things it gives you is a lack of fear. It teaches that there is a place for you. Whenever I lost an audition I'd say, 'All right, that wasn't yours. Forget it!' I've never been jealous of another performer. There is room for every single person in the world."

Carol also has other fond memories of her grandmother:

"She was a character. I could go anyplace I wanted to. Do anything I wanted. She never checked on me. If I said I was going over to a girlfriend's house and wasn't going to be back until the next morning, Grandma offered no objection. But I'd go to the girlfriend's house and I'd be back the next morning just as I had promised. I didn't fool around or anything like that. And that kind of helped me grow up and mature more quickly. I learned responsibility."

Meanwhile, across the hall, Carol's younger sister was growing up under Mama's wing. Although Mrs. Burnett continued her bouts with the bottle, her alcoholic binges didn't inflict any severe hardships on Christine during her formative years.

"The only way Chris had ever known Mama was—loaded," Carol says. "But Mama also knew how to raise a child whether she was in her cups or not. . . ."

That's the story of the very early part of her life as I have gotten it from Carol Burnett, as perhaps a score or more other reporters have also gotten it from her. But her uncle, Tex Burnett, was willing to divulge to me some family background that Carol has never publicly talked about. He doesn't believe his niece has been as kind as she could have been to her parents, as she has so often stressed the seamy side of their lives.

"I don't blame Carol for her claims that she was the child of chronic boozers and that she grew up in poverty," Tex Burnett said, conceding that her parents had made mistakes. "So if she really said those things she said them because she thought they were so. She's always been that kind of kid—straightforward, honest, even guileless. I know she wouldn't deliberately stretch the truth for publicity's sake, and she certainly wouldn't stretch it at the expense of an unhappy couple who loved her: her weak, handsome, totally charming father and her brilliant, beautiful mother."

Tex Burnett attributes Carol's talents—her creativity and showmanship—to her genealogy; they are family traits, inherited from a long procession of forebears who were in one aspect or another of show business. Her paternal grandfather, Joseph Hiram Burnett, was with the Gentry Brothers Circus and wrote the musical scores for the animal acts.

Carol's other uncle, John Burnett, was in the movie business back in the days of one-and-two-reelers. John was a pioneer producer of sorts. He filmed cowboy-and-Indian pictures on the 101 Ranch in Oklahoma and toured that state and Texas screening them. In fact, he'd also dress like a cowboy or an Indian and ride a horse into each town where the pictures were playing to drum up an audience. Afterward, he went to the University of Texas and studied journalism, then took off for Hollywood and became publicity man for the *Cathay Circle Theater.*

"If Carol's uncle John hadn't been interested in the movies and gone to Hollywood," said Tex Burnett, "my niece's entire life would have been different—and the tragic lives of her parents as well. That old saying that there are a million broken hearts for every light on Broadway fits Carol's parents perfectly. Their hearts were broken by their quest for success in Hollywood."

Carol's father, Jody, had a lot of flair and showmanship of his own, inherited from his father, Joseph, the circus lyricist. In fact his aunt Abbie, Carol's great-aunt, was a pianist who played concerts in Texas on a grand piano that she'd hauled all the way from Tennessee. Jody's own interest in Hollywood and a penchant for a film career were stirred by his brother John's pursuits in the movie capital.

"Jody was a nice-looking kid," Carol's uncle Tex said. "Girls liked him. In fact he was spoiled. So, inevitably, he thought he could be a star. Carol remembers her father, of course, but she couldn't have remembered him when he was at his best. He was the baby of the family, our mother's darling, the boy who could do no wrong. He grew too fast and, maybe because of that, he was always sick. In fact, he had double pneumonia two or three times while he was a child. That probably weakened his lungs and caused him to contract tuberculosis in the later years of his life. However, even though he was spoiled and petted, he was a likable youngster who was too good-natured and gullible for his own good."

Uncle Tex had an imaginary imp who performed magic for him. When anyone lost something, he'd pretend that his imp was going to lead him to whatever was lost and, sure enough, Uncle Tex would go right to the missing object.

"Jody was mystified and really believed in my imp," Tex Burnett explained. "He believed in it so strongly that I sold it to him for a pocketknife. But then he complained that the imp wouldn't do any magic for him, and yet he never did figure out that he'd been cheated."

That incident, observed Carol's uncle, had great significance. It may have been the first time that Jody made a bad bargain because he believed too firmly in magic.

"Jody still believed in magic when he met Carol's mother, Louise, while they were in high school," Tex Burnett went on. "I don't think there was ever between them the stuff from which good, solid marriages, lasting relationships, are made, but I'm sure they thought they were in love."

Tex Burnett said he couldn't say enough good about Carol's mother—how pretty and sweet she was when Jody first met her. Louise, according to Tex, was a brilliant woman.

Because Jody's luck had always been so good in his early youth, he may have become blind to the possibility that he could someday run into disaster. His alcoholism aside, bad things just didn't happen to Jody Burnett. His good fortune continued even after high-school graduation when a friend with important connections in a small town outside of Houston got him a job as a health officer—for an astounding two hundred and fifty dollars a month.

"Getting that job was one of the worst things in the world that could have happened to my brother," Tex Burnett believed. "Not only was the salary magnificent, completely unrealistic in the nineteen twenties for a boy fresh out of high school, but Jody's duties were practically nonexistent. About all he had to do was look nice, make a good impression on people, and be able to hold his liquor. His success with all three strengthened his impression that nothing could darken his future.

"I guess Jody could have kept that job in Texas indefinitely," Carol's uncle went on. "But California kept

14

drawing him like a magnet. So he moved to Los Angeles and got a job as a soda jerk. He and several boys shared an apartment there and staged pie fights, practicing for the day when they would be big Hal Roach stars."

But Miss Burnett's father never got inside the studio. Suddenly the breaks that had always come his way stopped coming. Meanwhile, back in Houston, Louise got lonesome and followed Jody to California. At every stop she wired to let him know her progress. Uncle Tex vouched for that because he'd seen the telegrams.

"I know Carol has been infatuated and she has been in love, so she must know how her mother felt," Tex said. "She was young and inexperienced, and she had the innocent idea that if she could just get to Jody they'd live happily ever after."

Louise and Jody, according to Carol's uncle, married without giving their future a single serious thought. They spent their honeymoon in Tex's apartment on Wilshire Boulevard, sleeping on a mattress that was laid across chairs in the living room. The year was 1932 and the country was in the deepest throes of the Depression. But Tex, working for $47.50 a week as an engineer, managed to help keep other members of the Burnett family from starvation. Jody was unemployed and so was his other brother, John.

Tex Burnett had both his brothers and their wives living in his small apartment. Finally Jody got disgusted waiting for a break in movies and decided to return to Texas. He took Louise to San Antonio—and the next year their first daughter, Carol, was born.

"Those early years in San Antonio were happy ones for Carol," Tex remembered with far greater recall for detail than his niece has exhibited in her recitals about those times. "She had all the care and attention a little girl could ever want. Her father, working as manager of that theater, earned a respectable livelihood. There was no painful poverty for Carol, nor did she suffer from want and neglect. The pictures I have of her show a plump, happy, well-dressed little girl who doesn't appear to be

15

suffering from anything. The bad times that made such an impression on her came much later. When she was small, her father wasn't drinking and was working, and he loved her very much."

Although Carol Burnett feels that alcohol was the villain in her parents' downfall, Tex Burnett said that that wasn't the real culprit—it was Hollywood, the fascinating yet cruel, unpredictable town.

"Ironic, isn't it?" Tex said. "Hollywood destroyed her parents and then helped make Carol an internationally famous star! She attained the stardom that her father had hoped for—and that even I had a flickering dream of achieving."

Tex spent his early years in Hollywood in show business. He had scored a small success in a radio program of his own for a while, then he played in *Wings*, the 1927 Paramount production which starred Buddy Rogers and Richard Arlen—and also featured an up-and-coming future superstar named Gary Cooper.

While managing a theater provided a good living for Jody, Hollywood was so irresistible that he just couldn't stay away. His determination to break into movies was still an obsession. So Jody and Louise went back to the film capital, bringing their eight-year-old daughter, Carol, with them. But studio doors were still closed to Jody Burnett.

Uncle Tex filled us in on one of Carol's father's experiences, a vicarious taste of glamor which only increased his thirst for movie-acting:

"He got a job handling traffic at a big tennis tournament attended by the stars. Jody himself was driving an old, beaten-up car that he called Homer. But he got a kick out of seeing the chauffeured Rolls-Royces and Packards that brought the celebrities to different places.

"During the tournament, Gary Cooper came up to him and asked for his car—he wanted to drive to where his own chauffeur-driven car was waiting for him. Jody was never timid, so he said, 'Mr. Cooper, I think the best way for us to handle this would be for you to get in my car with me, and I'll drive you to yours.'

"Cooper climbed into Homer and let Jody drive him, rattling and bouncing along on two flat tires, to his limousine."

More often, Jody Burnett did less interesting work, like selling radios, which wasn't the kind of goal Louise expected her husband to reach. She had higher ambitions in Hollywood for her husband as well as for herself.

"Louise was a very pretty woman, as I said," Uncle Tex declared, revealing a side that Carol never spoke about to reporters. "She was a smart one, too. When people noticed this and told her how pretty and smart she was, she was naturally flattered and she began to want more than her husband could provide. Not just money, but more excitement, more parties, and more fun in general."

By then Louise had landed a job doing publicity for one of the studios and, according to Uncle Tex, that put her in touch with a pretty lively crowd.

"Maybe if Carol tries hard she can recall how the new friends finally won her mother away from her father entirely," Tex said with bitterness. "And that was the beginning of the bad times that Carol seems to remember so vividly in all the stories she has told about her childhood.

"The real story is that perhaps Carol didn't go to the Riviera or Acapulco, but she did know what the white sands of Santa Monica Beach were like. Her parents took her there very often. She didn't ever know poverty. Unhappiness at times, yes. Especially after Louise and Jody separated."

After the separation, Tex said, Jody began going downhill physically, financially, and every other way. At the beginning Carol stayed with her aunt. But then she settled with grandmother White. Tex also disclosed some of the acrimony that developed in the family after the breakup:

"My mother and Carol's grandmother didn't get along too well because each blamed the other's child for the

17

wrecked marriage. So while Carol was staying with her maternal grandmother in Hollywood, Jody and his mother were living in Santa Monica. And I know Carol had to be pretty subtle in order to get down there to see her father, whom she loved dearly."

Her visits to her father were frequent. He'd take her to the beach that they once enjoyed as a family, and he'd take her to the movies, which she loved. But as the years passed her visits lost their joy, for her father was drinking more and more.

"That must have been a horrible ordeal for Carol," Tex said. "She'd arrive in Santa Monica and find her father drunk—really roaring drunk. And then she'd go home and find her mother had gone out with her exciting friends. By that time neither her father nor her mother was supporting her, so I suppose she could, in all fairness, think of herself as poor. She wore clothes handed down by her Vance cousins, and that probably contributed to her inferiority complex.

"I know that in high school she had crushes on various boys, but she didn't dare hope that one could really like her. She felt unloved and unlovely. She felt like Cinderella sitting in the ashes."

One day, Uncle Tex said, he shared an experience with Carol that was somewhat like the Cinderella story—it even involved a pair of slippers, although they weren't of glass.

Tex had stopped at Mrs. White's to see how Carol was. She said she was going to the junior prom that night. It occurred to her uncle that Carol probably didn't have any evening dress other than something handed down from her cousins.

"Do you have something to wear?" he asked.

"Oh, yes, sure," Carol answered, "I'm fine—except I do need some evening shoes."

"Come on, then," Uncle Tex invited, "we'll go get some."

So off they went to downtown Los Angeles, shopping.

"Before we got home," related Tex Burnett, "we'd

18

bought shoes, a dress, an evening wrap, and whatever else a girl needs to be beautiful at a dance. She thanked me so quietly that I wasn't sure she really wanted the things and, after we went into the house, she slipped off into her room without saying another word.

"I talked with her grandmother a few minutes and got ready to leave. Before going, I tiptoed back to Carol's room to speak to her. I heard her sobbing through the door."

"What's the matter, honey?" Uncle Tex asked.

"Matter?" Carol replied. "Oh, nothing's the matter. I'm just crying because the clothes are beautiful. Do you know, all I'd planned to do was to con you out of a pair of shoes."

Tex laughed. "You see, she felt so insecure that she thought she'd have to 'con' someone to get her shoes. It never occurred to her to come right out and ask for help from the people who loved her."

Perhaps that wasn't so surprising. Carol's uncle admitted that he hadn't taken as much interest in his niece as he should have, and neither had her other relatives. That, he added, was purely carelessness on their part. They didn't do more only because they just didn't think about it—seems they were always too busy doing something else.

Yet Uncle Tex feels that his niece should show more compassion for her parents when she talks about them with interviewers. His point was:

"Carol's father, her mother, and all the rest of us were about like most people—human."

Isn't it strange that Carol Burnett, in all the many years she has been talking with reporters, has never mentioned any of these anecdotes provided by her uncle?

When she is asked to relive her early childhood, time and again she rehashes the same line—the poverty, her parents' drinking, how miserable it was for her most of the time.

So far as I know—and I've researched her life thoroughly—Carol has never talked to any reporter about her uncle Tex and the fact that he played in a movie, about her Grandpa Joe writing musical scores for a circus, her uncle John being an early moviemaker, or her great-aunt Abbie performing as a pianist in concerts.

Nor has Carol ever spoken of those happy days with her parents on the Santa Monica Beach that Tex described —nor a word about the day Tex helped Carol become Cinderella.

Dorothy Kilgallen once said about Carol: "She is about as unphony and normally blueberry pie as you can get and still stay in show business."

But later Edith Efron, writing in *TV Guide*, observed:

"On the other hand, those who deal closely with her often claim that her 'blueberry pie' normality is illusory. Her eager dedication to her career seems to be an iron wall that cuts her off from most of reality. A systematic query of her associates reveals the peculiar fact that no one has ever heard Carol Burnett converse in a sustained fashion on any subject which does not relate in some way to the entertainment world." Ms. Efron then quoted Garry Moore, who helped boost Carol to stardom: "I don't believe we've talked more than two pages worth of anything but show business since I've known her."

When Carol was still a little girl, living with her grandmother, she took progressively greater interest in school as she advanced from one class to another. Reading was a large part of her interest. Or, as Carol puts it:

"Books were important to me as a kid. I will never forget how impressed I was with *The Yearling*. My sixth grade teacher had read that to us. She read it with such emotion that it meant more to me than *Hamlet*, which I read later on, in college. The warmth about the family was gripping, really. The kid's name in it is Jody, which was Dad's name" (and which also is Carol's middle daughter's name). "I don't know why but I just identified with that story. And when it opened as a movie I was the first one in line. It was the first time I went to a first-class movie house."

Carol saw the picture at Graumman's Egyptian Theater on Hollywood Boulevard.

"I really had to save up my money for the box-office admission that time," Carol recalls.

She also loved Grimm's fairy tales.

"They were pretty frightening, but I wasn't scared when I read them. What those stories made me do was start drawing fairy-tale scenes. That became a big pastime with me. I guess because I had always wanted to draw. I did pencil sketches."

In her early schooldays she was going to be "the greatest artist that ever lived."

"I used to hurry home from school and draw for hours. Even when I was four I had a pencil callus."

Carol recalls the job her grandmother had at Warner Brothers' art department—night cleaning woman.

"Grandma would take me along and I would leave samples of my drawings around hoping to be *discovered*. The art staff finally left a note for Grandma: 'Please leave art supplies alone!'"

Later Carol's passion became running.

"I had one prowess the boys admired. I could outrun them. I used to get up at six o'clock and play games with the neighborhood boys until dark. I invariably had skinned knees. My gym teacher even began thinking of the Olympics, and wrote a letter to my grandmother offering special coaching. But Nanny thought it wouldn't be good for me and said no."

Carol also has fond recollections of a family parakeet which her mother often nourished with whiskey and which kept repeating petulantly, "Where the hell have you been?" It seems, again, that Carol Burnett's most vivid memories of her childhood revolve around her parents' drinking:

When a classmate remarked that Carol's grandmother had exceptionally pretty legs and asked, "Did she get them from dancing?" Carol replied candidly, "No, she got them from making the run." (The "run" was the trip to the neighborhood liquor store for her mother's stock, Carol explained.)

During her years in Hollywood High School Carol discovered that her best grades invariably were in English. Carol devoted her efforts to a career in journalism by joining the staff of the school's newspaper. She wrote her own column of humor and verse. She was going to be a journalist—and, of course, would go to college to achieve that goal.

Her chances were excellent, for Carol's report card for her senior year shows a multitude of A's. She graduated with honors and planned to go on to the University of California at Los Angeles.

For many reasons Carol was happy to leave her high school years behind. For her pictures in her middle-teen years show a tall, somewhat gangly girl (she achieved her present five-foot-seven height at the age of eleven). Carol herself says about her insecurity with boys:

"I was still very athletic in high school and the boys all liked me—but when they wanted to ask a girl for a date, well! Having a steady, of course, was the living end. I got crushes all during high school, always on the most popular boys. You shoot for the moon. But *they* never knew it. At dances I'd rush to the ping-pong tables to hide the fact nobody was going to ask me to dance."

Carol Burnett explains her outlook for the future and why she set out to fulfill her goal by going to college:

"I had thought that I might become a newspaper or magazine writer. I also considered the possibility that I might become a playwright. Although I'd never really been turned on by the idea of being a journalist, I guess I had been influenced by my mother, who had written a little herself (and obviously well enough to write for the publicity department of a major Hollywood movie studio such as Warner's). Mom would say that it didn't matter altogether what you looked like so long as you could write. So I decided that that made sense and I enrolled as a journalism major at UCLA."

In an interview with Neal Gilkyson Stuart published in

Ladies' Home Journal in 1963 Miss Burnett told the writer that once she got to UCLA, she found there was no journalism department for undergraduates, and she entered the theater-arts department instead because it offered a course in play-writing. (If you're wondering how a girl from a broken home and in a state of financial deprivation could get into college, the answer is quite simple. Carol made it to UCLA because tuition for a semester cost a mere forty-two dollars!)

"I found a most astonishing thing," Carol said. "The curriculum I had signed for included an acting class. I wasn't particularly anxious to take the course although I had always liked acting, but I took the course because I had to have it to get my credits. You know what I think? I think I wanted to be an actress all along."

The UCLA drama-class professor assigned her to study the waitress's soliloquy from *The Madwoman of Chaillot*.

"I was a bust in that one," Carol admits.

Her acting debut in front of the drama class was indeed inauspicious if not devastating. She recited the lines in a dazed and scarcely audible monotone while moving her right hand mechanically back and forth in what she hoped was an imitation of a waitress wiping a lunchroom counter. Many of her classmates, not catching the words, thought she was portraying a slightly abnormal housewife at the ironing board. Although a charitable man, her professor gave Carole a D-minus.

Another time she chose a passage from *Petrified Forest*. The first line read, "Are you going to try to make me?"

"I was embarrassed to emote while I said the line," Carol grants. "So I mouthed it without any expression whatsoever."

That dead pan performance made the class roar with laughter; Carol got the idea right then and there that she could be a comedienne.

"At least I had discovered that I could be funny," Carol said.

Then came a class performance in which boys and

girls were paired off for skits. The more talented members of the class latched on to each other. Carol waited and, like the last kid on the block when they're choosing up sides, found that her partner was another outcast, Dick DeNeut, who planned a career not in acting but directing. The two waifs, stuck with each other, undertook the cheerless task of trying to compete with their betters. They performed a comedy sketch and Carol spoke but two words on stage. They got a flat C for that effort.

"But the class had roared," Miss Burnett related. "From that moment I was hooked. Nobody will ever know how good I felt. When I heard them laugh when they were supposed to, that was the biggest thrill and turn for me. I went home and said that I was going to be an actress. My mother took another drink and said, 'You're crazy. What do you mean you're going to be an actress?' I said, 'I know it. They felt it. They laughed.' And she said, 'Of course they laughed.' I said, 'No, they were supposed to.' Mama just didn't understand."

It was a Saturday night, June 12, 1954. Carol, having finished her junior year at college, was invited to an end-of-the-semester party by UCLA's music department. Another guest was Don Saroyan, a classmate of Carol's and a cousin of author William Saroyan. They had been summoned to the bash, a high-society garden party in San Diego, to provide entertainment with a scene from *Annie Get Your Gun*. Carol had Ethel Merman's role. An earlier happening had led to Carol's designation for the part:

"I had gotten to be gung-ho about doing musicals, although I couldn't read music," Carol said. "I didn't know I had a loud voice until it just kind of happened. A friend of mine had asked me if I could carry a tune. He wanted to know if I'd be in the chorus of a scene from *South Pacific*. Sure, I said. So we rehearsed, with me doing the segment of 'I'm Gonna Wash That Man Right Out Of My Hair.' But then I was put in a scene from *Guys and Dolls*,

24

and suddenly I wanted to be Ethel Merman and be on Broadway."

Then a remarkable thing happened at that San Diego festivity. A man who looked to be about fifty, and whose ancestry Carol guessed was either Italian or Filipino, approached her and Don after the *Annie Get Your Gun* performance. He spoke in broken English.

"He was also a little bit under the weather because he had had a few too many drinks," Carol said. "But he asked Don and me what plans we had. We told him that we wanted to go to New York City and study dramatics because anyone, even if that person looked like Marilyn Monroe or Tony Curtis, would still have to leave Hollywood and go somewhere else to be discovered."

The interrogator, who happened to be a wealthy building contractor, asked Carol and her handsome, dark-haired beau what they'd need to get that start.

"I told him that, frankly, the only thing that could help us was money," Carol said. "The man had raved and ranted about our performance on the stage and had told us that he was sure we could make it all the way to the top. And he explained that when he first came to this country he had dug ditches, but then made his fortune in post-War construction. Then he asked us to come see him in his San Diego office. We said we'd be there, but we'd call first."

Carol went home that night and thought about the man's offer. As she lay in her Murphy bed, her clothes still dangling from their hangers on the bathroom rack, she couldn't help but let her mind wander over the recent past. She reviewed her summer jobs in Hollywood, all of them so close to the stage yet so far away. One of those jobs was as usherette at Warner's Hollywood Theater.

"They were playing Hitchcock's *Strangers On a Train* and I saw it ninety times. I got fired because I wouldn't seat a couple who came in ten minutes before the end of the picture. I told them it would spoil it for them and that they should wait for the next show."

Carol also had a job at the Iris Theater as relief cashier at the box office. She recalls:

"They were showing *Ivanhoe* and the manager had the sound track piped into the cashier's booth so the passersby would hear it and maybe get interested enough to buy a ticket. I know the entire dialogue and all the sound effects, but I've never seen the picture because I don't think I could take it without ear plugs. Boy, do I know where that armor clanks!"

On Monday morning, June 14, 1955, Carol and Don—who were in love, if you haven't already guessed—phoned and then went to see the wealthy contractor. Carol describes the scene:

"We had thought that he'd had too much to drink when he had talked with us and laid down his proposition of help the previous Saturday night. Don and I figured that by Monday he'd have forgotten everything. Yet when we met him in his office he had a complete recollection of what he had promised. But he established strict provisions and restrictions about the help he was going to give us." (Carol and Saroyan were forbidden from ever revealing their benefactor's identity.) "He had called in his accountants and ordered two one-thousand-dollar checks drawn up. One was for Don and the other for me. The loan was for five years and it was to be paid back without interest. It had to be used to go to New York and to make an effort toward breaking into show business. Afterward, Don and I were committed to help others get ahead just as the man had helped us," Carol explained.

"We'll send you a regular report on how we're making out," Carol promised the contractor.

"Oh, hell," the benefactor shot back, "just send me a postcard once a year—a Christmas card. And I know you'll pay back. Others have."

"Has anyone gotten a fairer deal than that?" Carol asks. She provides her own answer:

"It was unbelievable, like a fairy tale. If a writer had tried to put that in a TV script, he'd have been ridden out

26

of the studio. Yet that was exactly what happened to Don and me."

Carol Burnett and Don Saroyan were ready now for New York. . . .

2

It wasn't until two months later that Carol Burnett actually boarded the Greyhound bus on that cross-country trek to the bright lights of Broadway in search of the theatrical success that Hollywood had not offered. The summer had imposed one of the first of life's severest heartbreaks on Carol Burnett: Jody, her father, had died.

"He was only forty-six years old," Carol said. "Although my parents were separated, I had always been very close to both of them. Of course, I had tried to help Mom and Dad. I had pleaded with them often to cut out their drinking. But no one in the family could really do it for them. They had to do it themselves. They were the ones who had to realize that they had hit the bottom. But they didn't. . . ."

Carol's uncle Tex had a different recollection of Jody Burnett's last years of life, and a very vivid memory about his death:

"Carol had already gone off to New York and I went back to Texas on business. Then I got a call saying that my brother John had dropped dead of a heart attack. I rushed to Los Angeles to make funeral arrangements and learned, when I got there, that Jody, who'd been released as cured after spending six years in a tuberculosis sanitarium, had caught a cold and developed double pneumonia. Jody died so quickly that I buried Carol's uncle and her father within the same week."

One thing worried Tex Burnett after this family double tragedy:

"Carol never once asked me where her father was buried. Maybe she's asked somebody else; maybe she's put flowers on his grave. But if she has it's news to me. As far as I know, her only memorial to her father was a magazine article that I read. She spoke of him bitterly, unkindly. Even if the quotes attributed to her were accurate, I'm not blaming her for them. I'm blaming myself, because it's my fault she didn't know the full facts about her parents sooner. It's time now, though, to set the record straight. Jody and Louise made plenty of mistakes—we all did—but when you reach my age you can look back on mistakes with understanding and compassion."

In Carol's account of the events surrounding her father's death she states that she remained at home after the funeral because her mother had taken ill and wasn't able to care for Christine. Although her sister was then nine years old, Carol didn't want to burden her grandmother with the chore of caring for a sick daughter and looking after a frisky, growing granddaughter.

In August, when Louise Burnett had recovered from her sickness, Carol decided that the time had come to strike out on her theatrical career in New York. Meanwhile, some of the one thousand dollars Carol had received from the wealthy immigrant contractor had been spent. When she was finally ready to go, Carol found that leaving wasn't all that easy.

"Nanny didn't want me to leave. She said that maybe something would turn up for me in the movies. But I had set my sights on the Broadway stage and no amount of persuasion was going to stop me now from going after what I wanted."

Neither Mrs. Burnett nor Mrs. White had a legal leg to stand on had they tried holding Carol back. She was already twenty-one. But neither her grandmother nor her mother even so much as suggested that Carol couldn't leave home.

"The only thing Nanny said to me was that if I wasn't a star by Christmas, to come right straight home. She told me, 'Either they like you or they don't like you.'"

Before Carol left, her grandmother had one request:

"She said, 'If you ever get on television, say hello.' I told Nanny that greeting friends was a no-no on TV. So she said, 'Then give me some kind of a signal that you know I'm here.'"

Carol was walking down the stairs lugging her single suitcase on her way to the bus station when she turned to her grandmother and said, "Okay, you watch me. When I get on TV, I'll say hello by pulling my left ear."

More than a year was to pass before Carol Burnett had an opportunity to appear on TV and to give her grandmother a private salute—the now-famous tug of her left earlobe.

"It happened on my first appearance on the *Paul Winchell Show* a year from the following December," Carol said. "When I pulled my earlobe, Nanny got the message."

Carol spent thirteen weeks with the ventriloquist on the NBC-TV network and it was her first stepping stone to success. But that was still sixteen months in the future in that late summer of 1954. Carol rode the Greyhound to New York alone. Don Saroyan, who was pursuing a master's degree at UCLA, had decided to stay awhile longer in California and finish his studies.

"It's a good thing that I had at least one friend in New York when I arrived," Carol relates.

The friend was a UCLA classmate, Eleanor Ebbie, who was living at the Rehearsal Club, a residence for hopeful actresses on Fifty-third Street in Manhattan. But Carol didn't head straight for the club:

"I'd heard so much about the Hotel Algonquin being the hostelry frequented by the theatrical elite that I decided to stay there," said Carol.

But after registering she learned, to her dismay, that

her room was going to cost nine dollars a day. Carol decided to dispense with such luxury. She phoned Eleanor, who invited Carol to come over to the Rehearsal Club. The girls agreed that they could live as roommates and got themselves billeted in a room that cost a modest eighteen dollars a week—and that even included meals.

"It was a little more difficult to find a job in a Broadway show than I had expected," Carol said. "I had wanted to get something in the chorus. I almost landed a part, but they didn't accept me in the end because I couldn't read music."

When the thousand dollars from her benefactor was nearly exhausted, Carol decided to look for a job in another field. She found work at Susan Palmer's Restaurant on Forty-ninth Street in Rockefeller Center.

"My job was hatcheck girl. But this restaurant happened to be a ladies' tea room. How many ladies do you know who check their hats? That's how bright I was."

But Carol, as a hatcheck girl, made quite a lasting impression at Susan Palmer's. The main dining room was on the street level and an oyster bar was downstairs. The restaurant under that name is no longer in existence, but the memory of Carol Burnett working as a hatcheck girl can never be forgotten by some of the longtime patrons of that establishment. One such patron—who happens to be a man—said:

"I would usually eat there when I was in a hurry. I could run downstairs, hang my hat and coat on a hook, and eat fast. But suddenly this girl with the teeth showed up at the checkroom upstairs. She struck like a rattlesnake. One minute I'd be dashing down those stairs, in the clear, and the next moment she'd be beside me, grabbing my coat. I had no intention in the world of ever checking my coat—there were all those lovely free hooks downstairs, and a quarter is a quarter—but half the time she'd outwrestle me for it."

Carol Burnett fought for tips as she fought for fame. She managed to earn an average of thirty dollars a week in tips, which supported her residency at the Rehearsal

Club. But things got a bit more hairy after Don arrived in New York.

"He stayed at a rooming house across the street," Carol said. "But when he couldn't break into show business he got a job as an usher at the Roxy Theater. That's as close as either of us got to the stage door."

Don's take-home pay was hardly better than Carol's. Moreover, his room didn't come with board. But Don never went hungry because Carol smuggled food out of the Rehearsal Club to her beau. Whenever those pickings got lean, Susan Palmer's served as an alternative source— Carol carried Don's nourishment out of the restaurant in doggy bags.

Meanwhile, Carol and Don spent every free moment making the rounds of theatrical agency offices. The responses and reactions Carol got became discouragingly monotonous.

"Always the same stock answer came from the agents for nearly a year and a half," Carol said. "They wanted to see me work professionally. But every kid knows this is the hardest nut to crack. How can you show your work if you can't get a job?"

Before Carol had left home she had set a time limit for herself to make good. If she didn't make it by then, she promised herself, she'd return to California.

"I gave myself five years. I vowed that if I wasn't earning a living—and to me earning a living would have meant any job in the chorus—I wouldn't hack it in New York any longer than the limit I had set."

One agent among all the many she had approached had a unique thought for Carol. She doesn't remember his name but vividly recollects what he told her: "Why don't you put on your own show and get exposure that way?"

Carol returned to the Rehearsal Club enthused with the idea of doing just that. And since by now—mid-1955 —she had been elected president of the club, Carol had the necessary influence to inspire a bunch of the girls to go along with her in the scheme.

"We decided to do the show at one of the Rehearsal

Club meetings," Carol said, her voice tinged with pride. "At all the earlier meetings I'd been to, nothing was ever accomplished. Everyone simply aired complaints about how tough it was getting jobs in show business. Now we could do something positive."

With guidance from Don Saroyan, who wanted to be an actor but preferred to become a director or producer, the production rapidly became reality.

Don slotted two dozen girls into the various skits and sketches for a two-hour variety show that he dubbed *Rehearsal Club Revue of 1955*. He rehearsed the cast—many of Carol's dormitory mates were skeptical and somewhat reluctant costars—for weeks, and finally the troupe was ready to perform.

The Rehearsal Club enjoyed a certain amount of prestige because so many stars had once boarded there, so it wasn't too difficult to entice a number of important theatrical figures to view the performance in Fischer Hall, which the girls had rented with their own money.

On opening night no fewer than two hundred and fifty agents, producers, and friends, many of them prodded from the rear, showed up.

"I did two acts in the show," Carol said. "In the first, another girl and I played twelve-year-old boys, which drew a barrel of laughs. In the second act I satirized Eartha Kitt by singing her hit 'Monotonous.' "

The scene was oh, so sexy. Sexy? Well, the stage was littered with all the accoutrements for such an atmosphere: chaise longues, etc. But Carol wasn't exactly made up to fit that setting nor to project the sensuous woman.

"I did my Eartha number in curlers and an old kimono. I knew I wasn't going to win any glamour prizes. I was going to have to establish myself as a slob."

How many of the girls landed jobs after this unique exhibition is something Carol will always remember—no fewer than fourteen girls were given work in show business.

Yet a couple of other benefits had also accrued: The Rehearsal Club's board of directors gave the girls the three hundred dollars needed to carry on their work for future productions, and then two more performances were staged in the months ahead, with more theatrical jobs opening for many of the girls. And in the end, Don got a job directing industrial shows and Carol landed an agent who found her immediate employment in a show in Chicago.

"It was an industrial show," Carol said with a squirm. "The job lasted a week. I was hired to plug aluminum foil and to sing ditties about what a wonderful product it was."

Back in New York after this shining triumph, Carol didn't have to pound the pavement from one theatrical agent to another: she had an agent already working for her. And she couldn't help but wonder what new worlds he was going to line up for her to conquer next.

"What step is there after you've done aluminum foil?" Carol asked. "Well, you can always push Planter's peanut oil. 'Ooh, how slippery it is . . .'"

Luckily for Carol, Arthur Willi, a partner of Martin Goodman Productions, was in the audience with his wife on the night the *Rehearsal Club Revue of 1955* was staged. Significantly, Goodman Productions, a group of theatrical agents, have always been very choosy about adding to their celebrated list. And Willi did not seem to be in a mood that night to represent any of the cast on the stage in Fischer Hall. But strong influences worked against his own judgment. Or, as Willi remembers that night:

"After the first act, before Carol's solo, I told my wife, 'I've had it. Let's hit the road.' She made me stay. When I saw Carol Burnett, I liked her. When I read what *Show Business Review* said about her" (Among other things, the writeup said, "Easily the winner . . . was Carol Burnett.") "I went after her."

Among the auditions that Willi worked out for Carol that spring were those held by Gus Schirmer, Jr., for summer stock. These were important auditions, and they commanded old hands and new hands as well as great

34

and small. It was Schirmer's practice to ask a young composer, lyricist, and theatrical coach named Kenneth Welch to play the piano during auditions.

Welch was about Carol's age and he had come to New York not long before her to write what he had expected to be *the* greatest musical comedy. But his multiple gifts and acute insight into people sidetracked him from that goal and he ended up in a rather technical specialty—creating the right material for performers and coaching them in it. Welch recalls his first encounter with Carol Burnett:

"In comes a girl I'd never heard of—just in from the West Coast. She was wearing a skirt and blouse. I must say, even before she performed I liked her. Once she started, I was enchanted. She sang 'How About You?' by Gershwin. It wasn't funny—it was young and fresh. I thought she was the greatest thing I'd seen in three years. She didn't get the job, incidentally. I have never done this before or since, but after the audition I followed her into the hall and said, 'I have to tell you this. I think you're absolutely brilliant.' She said, 'Thank you very much.' That was all. So I thought maybe I'd never see her again."

Carol landed a summer job playing in *Green Mansions* with a stock company. When she returned to New York City that fall and decided she needed professional help, someone recommended Ken Welch. She looked him up in the telephone directory and began, "You won't remember me . . ." The reply was, "Indeed I do. Come on up."

Carol has a vivid and warm memory of that encounter with Welch:

"I went up and Ken made me sing everything I knew. He observed that every time I sang a romantic ballad, with no girlish character to hide behind, down would come a mental block."

They talked—a conversation Carol still regards as one of the most important ones of her career.

"He searched out my aims. He found I was deadly serious about my career. He told me he could probably

35

prepare some far-out comedy that might make me the rage at a Greenwich Village night spot but would lead to a professional dead end."

Which did Carol Burnett want? Quick work at the moment or a real career which might take years to build?

"I told him I wanted musical comedy, the big time."

The discussion between Carol and Welch ended on the subject of money. Carol confided in Ken that she didn't have any. He told her that he believed in her future.

"I proposed to Ken that I come every second week for his professional coaching," Carol said. "Ken wanted me to come twice a week. 'No,' I told him, 'I don't want it that way.' "

Ken Welch remembers what happened next:

"I went to the dimestore and bought a book of blank promissory notes. That was my way of getting her to agree to come."

That was the beginning of a long relationship, for with very few exceptions, Ken would write Carol's material for a long time to come. Then, even as the lessons from Welch were continuing, she learned from Arthur Willi that he'd placed her in a romantic lead on an upcoming NBC-TV network series.

"I was the dummy's girlfriend on the *Paul Winchell Show*," Carol recalls with amusement. "My job was singing romantic ballads to Jerry Mahoney. Uhhh!"

That certainly beat the routine that occurred after Carol's return from promoting aluminum foil in Chicago —the summer job in the Adirondack Mountains resort doing walk-ons in *Green Mansions*. Yet, however inconspicuous and uninspiring those stints were, to Carol it was work in what she still considered her first love— performing on stage before a live audience. But the job as the dummy's girlfriend on Paul Winchell's show was something Carol had not expected; it changed her view about the immediate future.

"I still wanted to perform on the legitimate stage," Carol said, "but being on TV wasn't a bad deal. Especially since it was a network show."

Carol's role as second banana on Winchell's program gave her an opportunity to display her talents in a nationwide showcase, even though she was restricted to song. The result, however, was a sudden flood of gratifying tributes from viewers all over the country.

Fans raved about the lovable funny singer even though the exposure she received was limited. Viewers begged to see more of her. All the brass at NBC immediately tuned in on the Winchell program to see for themselves just what made the dummy's damsel such a hit.

"I didn't hear of anyone forming a Carol Burnett fan club then," Carol said, "but I was too excited and too preoccupied with other matters to entertain such thoughts."

One of her preoccupations was the deliberation she'd been giving to a matter that led to her decision to marry Don Saroyan. It happened on the very day she landed the part in Winchell's show—December 17, 1955.

By then Eleanor Ebbie, Carol's UCLA friend and roommate at the Rehearsal Club, had also made some gains in show business, and was living in Yonkers. The wedding reception for Carol and Don was held in Eleanor's house. A friend who requested anonymity spoke about the couple:

"They had no money and the car they had hired broke down. The marriage seemed ill-fated from the start."

That old saw which says love is blind might have been aptly applied to this marriage, and perhaps it was more befitting of Carol's attitude than Don's. The friend said further:

"Carol was very much in love with Don. But I'm not so certain he returned her love in kind. He was egocentric and not too infrequently he treated Carol like, well, you know, not good. When they were on the UCLA campus he would flirt with lots of girls and date quite a few of them. Yet he always gravitated back to Carol. On the other hand, Carol was always loyal to Don. She never betrayed any hurt those times when Don was off with some other girl, but I always sensed that inside Carol, who is very sensitive, must have suffered terribly."

In New York Don appeared to stop sowing wild oats. At least all indications are that he was totally devoted to Carol and was fully immersed in the advancement of her career—as well as his own whenever he found an opportunity to promote it.

Though Don didn't encounter much success in promoting himself, he managed to latch on to a few fairly good deals. His main thrust after Carol started making it in the big time was in the production of industrial films, which really wasn't what Don had wanted to do. (Eventually he would land an actor's role playing opposite Errol Flynn's girlfriend, Beverly Aadland, which we'll discuss later.)

"I enjoyed working on Paul Winchell's show," Carol said. "I thought I was getting somewhere. I loved the fan mail that flowed in."

The fan mail poured in only as long as the show lasted on the air—thirteen weeks. Despite the accolades for Carol which inundated NBC, the ratings based on the home-viewers' feelings about the program as a whole didn't reflect the same depths of affection. And the network was compelled to lower the guillotine on the *Paul Winchell Show*.

"Suddenly I was out of work again," Carol remembers with mixed emotions. "Although jobless, I was greatly encouraged by the experience and exposure I had gotten on Paul's show and I felt confident that I'd move on to something else. My preference still was to do something on the stage, but I wasn't going to fight it if another TV offer came along."

Her optimism was justified. Carol Burnett was due for more work—and for bigger and better roles. . . .

3

One of Carol's preoccupations since she'd first decided to pursue an acting career at UCLA was to meet Broadway producer-director George Abbott.

"I liked his ideas and the musicals he staged," Carol said in a tone betraying her total fascination with this great theatrical figure. "I promised myself that I would be in one of his shows someday."

In late fall of 1955, when she was between jobs, Carol divulged to a friend how she thirsted to work in a musical, even if only in the chorus. The friend suggested that Carol see her friend Eddie Foy, who was starring on Broadway in one of Abbott's smash musicals, *Pajama Game*.

"I took a deep breath, summoned all my courage, and headed for the theater," Carol explained. "To my surprise, Eddie Foy agreed to see me backstage." Then this exchange took place:

"How do you get to work in a musical?" Carol asked.

"Can you sing and dance?" Foy wanted to know.

"A little," Carol replied eagerly.

Foy gave Carol the name of an agent and told her to see him. He also promised to talk to the agent about her.

The next day Carol went to the agent's office, lugging her scrapbook of clippings reviewing her college skits. She didn't have any writeup for her walk-on in the Adirondack Mountains *Green Mansions* summer stock per-

39

formances nor for her Chicago stint in behalf of aluminum foil.

"The agent wasn't impressed with me and that was the end of that," Carol said.

It was after this disappointment that Carol looked up Ken Welch, after hooking up with Arthur Willi as her agent. And with her singing role on the *Paul Winchell Show* keeping her busy through the winter of 1955–56, Carol made practically no attempt to induce anyone to find work for her on the legitimate stage.

In March 1956, however, the Winchell program was flushed down the TV drain. But before she had pasted the clips of her thirteen-week TV experience into her scrapbook for another assault on Broadway, as she had planned, Carol received another video offer. Now they wanted her to play Buddy Hackett's girlfriend on his *Stanley* series, again on NBC.

At last Carol had an opportunity to do the sort of comedy she wanted to do—uninhibited farce befitting not the *female comic* but the *comedienne,* which was what she was striving to be.

"I never wanted to be a female clown, which I consider to be a woman comic," Carol explained. "A comedienne is different. She's an actress who does comedy parts."

But rehearsals and filming for the *Stanley* show were still some months away from fall. Now it was just the beginning of summer. Carol was between jobs. Don was miserable in his nonacting business-show whirl.

"Okay," she told him, "quit!"

And suddenly they were both receiving unemployment checks. Yet that summer was a happy one. Carol, Don, Ken Welch and his wife, a young singer named Mitzi, went off together to a resort in the Poconos, staging weekly free-wheeling skits.

With the Elvis Presley craze at its zenith then, Ken wrote a skit and a scorching torch song, *Destroy Me*, and Carol went on stage and performed. She was a smash in the role of a dowdy housewife singing to her unnamed idol.

Back in New York that fall, Carol began rehearsals for *Stanley*. For the first time Carol had the foundation on which she could build, a process that ultimately would turn her into the laugh machine that she is today—America's female Chaplin and one of the all-time funny women in the entertainment world. Her success is rooted in her own personal style, which she developed at UCLA and has never allowed anyone to alter:

"I'm not afraid to make myself unattractive. Most women are. There's all that training you've had since you were three. Be a lady! Don't yell or try to be funny! Just be a nice little girl. Sit quietly with your knees close together and speak only when you're spoken to. When I was a kid and crossed my eyes or screwed up my face, my mother whacked me. It's that kind of training and upbringing that discourages women from messing up their hair or keeps them from not wearing lipstick, slouching, looking flat-chested, or being unattractive in any way. Me? The sloppier I am, the more comfortable I am, the better I feel in a comedy sketch."

Whatever dreams Carol Burnett had of making herself into a premiere comedienne on Buddy Hackett's show went the discouraging route of the Paul Winchell venture. Again, Carol excelled and the fans lauded her antics (and Buddy Hackett's, too). But *Stanley* didn't tickle enough funny bones on the Nielsen ratings, and Carol was at liberty again.

But by then Carol didn't mind. Something wonderful had happened to her—she'd met Garry Moore and had been on his show. The beginning of that happy story goes back to a day in late summer of 1956 after Carol and Don and Ken and Mitzi had returned from the Poconos.

They got together one evening at Carol and Don's new apartment, at 142 West 54th Street. The furnishings were somewhat skimpy, for Carol and Don weren't yet rolling on easy street, but at least they weren't eating out of the old beanpot or snitching snacks from the Rehearsal Club or Susan Palmer's tea room.

At that gathering at Carol and Don's, Ken offered a suggestion.

"What a wonderful idea!" Carol exclaimed. "Audition for Garry Moore? Audition for Garry Moore! Wild!"

Welch had proposed writing a script for Carol, an act that would include a song about types who try out at auditions and in which she would play several parts. Ironically, the theme revolved about a girl auditioning for a Broadway show—which Carol had done, unsuccessfully.

"That seven-minute script that Ken prepared was all the material I had," Carol said as she relived that thrilling turning point in her career. "Garry was inside the glass-paneled control room. As I went through the audition, I couldn't hear his reaction. But I could see him laughing, and that put me at ease. When I finished, he came out and asked, 'Do you have anything else?' I swallowed hard. 'No, sir, that's it,' I choked. 'Okay,' Garry smiled, 'I want you on my show.' There was no 'Thankyouverymuch, we'llcallyou, don'tcallus' or any of that stale routine. Boy, was I happy!"

November 9, 1956, was the most significant early chapter of Carol's career. That morning she was a guest on Garry Moore's show—and she was a hit.

Because of the rib-cracking comedy she performed on that one-shot on the *Garry Moore Show*, she was called to appear on Ed Sullivan's Sunday night variety hour, and again she cracked the laugh meter. Suddenly Carol was even more in demand. Garry Moore wanted her back—and there was word that even Jack Paar was considering Carol for an appearance on his late-night NBC-TV talk show.

"Think of something unique and funny that she can do," Paar's program manager told Carol's agent, "and we'll have her on the show."

Yet that didn't happen until after Carol was signed to do a nightclub routine, her first such engagement. What made it an extra-special deal was that her cafe debut was to be at New York's renowned Blue Angel.

So far in her career, Carol had never allowed herself

a leer, a wiggle, or even a double entendre in any performance. Nightclub floors from coast to coast were littered with the bleached bones of male and female comics who had tried to be funny and clean. Carol Burnett was about to prove that she could be an exception.

"I was one of four twenty-minute acts at the Blue Angel," Carol reminisced. "I had a two-week contract and was obligated to do two shows nightly. I'd never worked a nightclub before, yet I knew the routines. Entertainers usually open in nightclubs with a 'Hello! Hello! We're glad to see you! We're glad you could be here tonight' type of song. I wasn't the headliner, I was the second act."

Ken Welch prepared Carol's material and she went over so well on her opening in early June of 1957 and for every night after that, to the delight of the management, that her two-week contract was extended to another four. At that point Ken Welch had to prepare new material.

For months he had mulled over his old housewife's love song, *Destroy Me,* never quite satisfied with it although it had gone over well in the Poconos when Carol had sung it.

"When you know Kenny, he's never satisfied," Carol said. "Kenny and I agreed that I had to have an opening number that would make the customers stop gabbing and listen to me. This was still the height of the rock 'n' roll craze and teenagers were still falling in love with Elvis Presley as if shot down by machine guns.

"Ken and I thought, Whom would it be funny for a teenager to fall in love with? We decided he had to be someone other than Presley. Ken said it had to be an absolutely absurd idol. We thought up a few names—like Khrushchev and Bulganin—but rejected them. Then Ken said, 'What about John Foster Dulles?' I thought it was a hysterical idea. Mr. Dulles was a fine man, but he was anything but a sex symbol. So Ken then wrote the lyrics."

Carol's comedy routine during the first two-week stand was funny enough. She kidded her way through a satire on TV's weather girls, whom no one had any trouble identi-

43

fying, and she did other comedy routines. The patrons had a rollicking good time with that, but when she returned with the love song to the Secretary of State, they choked on their drinks. The beguine-type song, called "I Made A Fool Of Myself Over John Foster Dulles," rocked the Blue Angel with laughter as never before. The lyrics opened with Carol in prison saying:

It's so nice of you all to come visit me here in prison.
I look forward to Friday . . . Friday is visiting day.
Would you like to know just why I'm here in prison?
I'm here because I'm classified as a threat to national security—top secret—first class—4-O—double A—and it happened this way:

After that introduction, Carol launched into song . . . Then Carol finished with more talk:

It's so nice of you all to visit me here in prison. With good behavior I should be out, oh, in about seven years. But I'm not un-American and I'm not a spy. But how can I convince the FBI that I'm simply on fire with desire for John Foster Dulles?

All hell broke loose after Carol's rendition of the song at the Blue Angel.

On the night of Tuesday, August 6, the *Jack Paar Show* called.

"Will you come over and do a song?" Carol was asked.

"What song?" Carol wanted to know.

"Your John Foster Dulles song," she was told.

"I don't think I should," Carol responded.

"Why not?" the man from Paar's talent office came back.

"For one thing it's political," replied Carol.

Of course the song wasn't political but Carol had a few apprehensions about doing the song on the air.

"I was afraid I might insult the Republicans, or some mixed-up Democrat might think I was on the Republican side," she said. "But I finally said yes. And I left the Blue Angel for a half hour and sang on the Paar show. By the time I got back to the club, a telephone call was waiting for me from the State Department. I thought,

This is it. I'm being deported back to Texas. I'm out of show business! On the phone was Mr. Dulles' TV consultant, David Waters. He said, 'I saw you. I heard it. I loved it.' I almost screamed, 'You did?' He said, 'Yes, and I hope you'll do it again.' It was crazy. Papers kept calling and wanting copies of the lyrics. I was asked to go to Washington to sing it for Mr. Dulles. I couldn't go that day, and he went off on a world trek, so I never met him."

David Waters didn't only phone Miss Burnett; the next day, Wednesday, he called NBC in New York and asked to have Carol sing the song again on television because the Secretary of State would certainly be seated in front of his set on that occasion. Waters also hinted that Dulles had an open spot in his busy schedule on Friday night.

So Jack Paar, not being one to turn down a "command performance," asked Carol if she'd do the honors again. And Carol did. However, while the State Department had reflected official amusement over the song, NBC received exactly the reaction Carol feared—one hundred and twenty-eight protesting calls from viewers who considered the renditions during the austere administration of President Dwight D. Eisenhower's years as something akin to diplomatic japery.

Yet that figure was wiped away by some twelve-thousand other calls cheering Miss Burnett's performance and begging the network to bring her back. NBC was now battling CBS for Carol, who had become the pet guest of network TV. So Carol found herself jumping from the *Jonathan Winters Show* to the *Ed Sullivan Show* and even to *Pantomime Quiz*, which was aired on the "third network," ABC-TV.

Her greatest exposure, however, was with Sullivan. Carol had appeared on his show in January and again on the Easter show, and then Ed asked her to return for three additional appearances starting in mid-August. And later that year, in November, Carol joined some of the biggest stars in the stage, movie, and television firmament for a shining special, *The General Motors 50th Anni-*

versary Show. Carol Burnett was being kept busy as a beaver.

"I was very lucky then," Carol offers. "I'm still very lucky today because I'm not a pusher. The things that have happened to me have been very fortunate. I was at the right place at the right time. Actually I'm very thin-skinned. I'm not a fighter. And if people were to give me the Bronx cheer or the raspberries, I'd shrink up."

Carol was petrified when she stepped on the Blue Angel stage on opening night. But she found a way of psyching herself to face the audience without trepidation.

"When I entered the club and saw those people sitting there, I felt every single one of them was an ogre, waiting to devour me," Carol remembered. "But as I dressed, I imagined all of them wearing silly long flannel nightgowns. They became a little ridiculous to me, rather than frightening. It worked. I stopped being scared."

The year 1957 had been very good for Carol Burnett. Yet it was only the beginning of her climb to premiere comedic stature. By year's end, Carol looked back on her accomplishments of the preceding twelve months and found that she would not have done anything differently— except perhaps that she would have liked to have made an even stronger assault on George Abbott.

She still wanted to play on the stage. Well, she'd give it a try again next year. Now Christmas was approaching and Carol hadn't been home in more than three years. It was about time to visit her mother, grandmother, and sister, Carol decided. And she went off to Hollywood.

"When I got home the first thing I noticed was that my sister was going in the wrong direction," Carol explained, setting the scene for the drastic action she was about to take. "I felt Chris was not being given the proper attention. I recognized that my mother wasn't going to last. I went to school to pick up Chris one afternoon and I didn't like the way she looked.

"We came home and I talked to my mother when she was in a kind of sober moment—we were closeted in the kitchen for three hours. I said to her, 'Let me bring Chris back to New York with me.' I told her it would be just for the Christmas holidays. But that wasn't exactly the truth. I intended to keep Chris with me. Mama cried. I think she knew she'd never see Chris again."

Carol brought her twelve-year-old sister to New York. Chris loved the big city and enjoyed staying with Carol and Don at their West Fifty-fourth Street apartment, which actually overlooked busy, seamy Eighth Avenue.

But then the holidays passed and Chris began to get homesick. Her mother had been calling Carol repeatedly, drunk and pleading, "I want my baby back." Carol finally convinced her mother that it was best to have Chris stay in New York. Yet Mrs. Burnett's capitulation was only half the battle. Chris didn't want to stay!

"When she said she wanted to go home," Carol said, "I told Chris that I wasn't going to let her go. She got hysterical. 'I have to go back!' she cried. 'I've got to go to school!' I told her, 'I'll put you in school here,' She wouldn't hear of it. Finally she pleaded, 'Let me call Mama.' I let her call. My mother said, 'Stay with Carol. It will be better.' And that was it. Chris stayed with me. Actually, you could say I kidnaped my kid sister from my mother."

As it turned out, ten days after that coast-to-coast phone conversation Carol received a call from her grandmother. It was January 10, 1958. Mrs. Louise Burnett had died. Her mother's death saddened Carol but it wasn't a shock, for she more or less expected it after seeing Mrs. Burnett's condition on that visit to Hollywood.

"Mom was all bloated. It was such a terrible shame. She had been such a pretty woman. She was forty-six when she died—the same age as my father. At least Mom had seen me on TV. Dad never had. I wished I could have done more to help my parents. But I had never been in a position to do that."

Even then, in early 1958, Carol's financial posture hadn't exactly reached Alpine heights. The biggest bundle she made in 1957—her only truly productive year up to that time—was from her six-week stand at the Blue Angel.

And a large part of those funds went into the furnishing of Carol and Don's apartment.

Had her parents lived, Carol is certain she could have helped them the way she would have wanted to.

"If I had one wish," Carol wants it known, "I would have wanted my parents to live long enough until I was making enough money to help cure them. I saw years ago that they had both lost their goals in life and they just found refuge in the bottle.

"Yet if I'd had enough to take care of them, I would have done it. I would have tried to send them someplace, to dry them out or to give them something to look forward to.

"But circumstances and fate conspired against that. I'm sorry they both died that way, but I can't blame myself for that. I am only sorry that I couldn't help them. . . ."

4

A flurry of favorable writeups surfaced in New York City's newspapers after Carol Burnett's sensational stand at the Blue Angel and her nationwide impact on Jack Paar's shows singing her love ballad to John Foster Dulles. But none of that publicity compared with the prestigious full-page spread in *The New York News* Sunday magazine section.

The story in America's largest-circulation daily appeared on October 13, 1957, and it was a solid barometer of Carol's arrival in the big time.

"Carol Burnett is a young comedienne who loves her husband, meat loaf with red gravy—and ice," the story started out.

"My ego shot up a thousand-fold when *The News* ran that story," Carol admits. "It was such a thrill to see myself in a quarter-page photo in my green lace see-through dress."

Another photo showed Carol sitting demurely on the couch of their apartment, with Don Saroyan squatting on the floor at his wife's feet. They had just begun to buy furnishings for their digs and one of the symbols of their newfound affluence was an eighty-five-dollar lamp which Carol and Don had coveted for months. They had spotted it in a midtown shop and, having no funds, employed various ruses to foil the salesman. Carol was quoted in the story:

"When we exhausted the line, 'No thank you, we're just looking,' we began buying cheap ashtrays. Soon our apartment began to look like a smokers' lounge. But when I got the job at the Blue Angel, Don and I streaked straight to the store and bought that lamp."

Perhaps the most fascinating aspect of the story was this quote from Carol:

"I don't smoke or like liquor, so I chew—ice. I load up my soft drinks with it and suck on the cubes as a chaser."

Of course that wasn't what she told Dick Cavett seventeen years later when she appeared on his ABC-TV talk show. Cavett, who induced Carol to talk about her parents' drinking problems, also got her to admit:

"I don't think it" (her parents' drinking) "affected me that much. I don't turn down any drink. I will have a drink. But I will certainly not be an alcoholic."

Although Carol had spoken about her parents' alcoholism on a few prior interviews, she had never mentioned the problem before on nationwide television.

"I'm not ashamed to talk about it," she told Cavett. "It's nothing to be shunned. As I said, drinking wasn't and isn't my problem. I know that sometimes it's inherited. But I'm not worried. I will never become an alcoholic."

Carol's weakness for meat loaf was discussed at length in that Sunday *News* feature. Writer Don Nelson let it be known that Carol's advancement to the Blue Angel had also elevated her gastronomic preferences to steak dinners. While Carol's success by then and the far greater strides she has made since have enabled her to afford the most sophisticated epicurean delights, her first love still is meat loaf with red gravy. Phenomenal success has changed her eating habits very little over the years.

"There are some foods I still don't like," Carol said, "like turnips or squash. I still approach new foods with some trepidation."

Carol has a favorite story about how she was introduced to a delicacy that she never imagined she'd ever work up the courage to try:

"It took Julie Andrews, Mike Nichols, my husband, and a couple of drinks to get me to try snails the first time. It was when Julie and I were performing together at Carnegie Hall.

"One night we went to dinner and I got brave and tried them for the first time. I kept remembering that line from the *Unsinkable Molly Brown* that goes something like—*eating snails would be good.* So I threw away my inhibitions. I adored them and loved sopping up the butter sauce with garlic bread."

No matter how many new foods Carol is introduced to, she always goes back to the meat loaf she learned to cook for Don, Chris, and herself in their modest Manhattan apartment.

Carol would like the world to have her recipe:

2½ pounds ground round
½ cup unseasoned bread crumbs
1 egg, beaten
½ green pepper, chopped
¼ cup sweet white onions, chopped
2½ tbsps. Worcestershire sauce
1 tsp. basil
½ tsp. oregano
⅛ tsp. garlic salt
½ tsp. seasoned salt
salt, freshly ground pepper to taste
1 cup milk
8 oz. can tomato sauce (or ¾ cup chili sauce diluted with water)

1. Put all ingredients except milk and tomato sauce (or chili sauce) in large mixing bowl. Squeeze meat mixture thoroughly with hands to blend well. Add

milk a little bit at a time, mixing well after each addition.

2. Line shallow baking pan with aluminum foil. Form meat into loaf in baking pan. Drizzle tomato sauce (or apply chili sauce as a glaze) over outer surface of the meat loaf.

3. Bake uncovered in preheated 300-degree oven about 1½ hours. Keep basting tomato sauce over loaf to keep it moist. (If chili sauce is used, basting is unnecessary). Serve with whipped potatoes, broccoli spears steamed with lemon butter, and tossed green salad.

Makes six to eight servings; leftovers can be frozen.

Those first few years of Carol's marriage to Don Saroyan were happy ones. Carol and Don had loads of laughs. She was very gullible then—and she still is:

"It's terrible. I'll believe anything. One day Don and I went for a ride. Suddenly he swerved the car. 'What's the matter?' I asked. So he said, 'I just wanted to avoid those tacks in the road.' Then he did it again and I got the same answer.

"So like a dope I hung my head out the window, scrutinizing the pavement for the tacks. It finally dawned on me when I turned around and saw Don howling. Can you imagine that?"

Afterward, when either Carol or Don would think the other was joshing about something, one or the other would ask, "Is this a tack?"

But that kind of fun didn't last very long. The tensions between Carol and Don began building, and finally they reached a point in their marriage when they saw no future together.

"We had begun having an ego problem," Carol says.

While Carol's star was ascending in 1958, Don was doing things he didn't want to do. Producing industrial shows wasn't his bag. He wanted greater rewards from his preparation for a professional career in the theater. He had a college degree and many hours invested toward his master's. His wife, who had quit UCLA after her junior year, was now a celebrity greatly in demand. Her income far exceeded anything he hoped to make in the foreseeable future. It wasn't a happy situation for Don—nor for Carol, who explains:

"The fact that I'd been successful far beyond anything I deserved did have something to do with it. What made it particularly rough was that Don wanted to be an actor too. If he'd wanted to be a director, as he had desired at the beginning, it wouldn't have been so hard. The fact that I was making more dough than Don didn't bug me, but it bothered him."

While Don was living the ego-damaging life of an actor nobody would hire, his wife was making another appearance on Ed Sullivan's Easter show, another guest spot on Mike Stokey's *Pantomime Quiz*, then on to a busy summer doing three *Chevy Show* guest spots on the West Coast, and even an engagement at the Desert Inn in Las Vegas.

When she returned home that fall Carol found that her occasional appearances on the *Garry Moore Show* were in peril. Because of its enormous popularity as a daytime show, CBS had decided to put it into a prime nighttime spot. But Garry's ratings didn't break through the roof. The network was considering canceling the show in January. And Carol had only one more date to perform for Moore.

"That was a low time," Carol said. "Then one day I met Garry's secretary on the street, and she told me Bob Banner was being brought in as producer. Bob had a magic touch. I knew Garry would have a hit."

And that's exactly how it turned out. In February 1959 the revived *Garry Moore Show* was aired; it became an instant hit. Carol had been scheduled to do only periodic guest appearances on the show, but fate brought her in on

53

the first night. She'd been summoned to pinch-hit for Martha Raye, who had taken sick. Carol went over smashingly, but still she wasn't taken on as a regular.

"Bob Banner said the show I did was great," Carol said. "But he's so thorough he waited until November to take me on as a regular:

Garry Moore explained why Carol finally had to be taken on as a regular:

"Our writers were begging for her. They were saying, 'This is a girl we'd love to write for.'"

Her designation as a regular on the *Garry Moore Show* elevated Carol to a new plateau of stardom but caused her marriage to become shakier—especially after she showed that her determination to perform on the legitimate stage was still undiminished, even in the face of the heavy grind week in and week out on the CBS sound stage.

Carol's video exposure led her to reason that her chances of landing a part in a Broadway show were now better than ever. And she'd heard that Richard Rodgers' *Babes In Arms* was being revived. She decided to try out.

"But I was turned down," Carol admits. "However, Bill and Jean Eckart, who were coproducing and designing sets and costumes for another musical, finally got me what I had been wanting all those years—an audition with George Abbott!"

Carol was terrified. It wasn't the first time that Abbott was seeing Carol. Although they'd never met, the producer had watched her perform in person on two prior occasions—not counting the times he might have seen her on TV.

"Sometime in 1958 I had been asked to perform at a Dutch Treat Club show, and I did," Carol said. "I also thought I had laid a bomb. It's dreadful to have to make an all-male audience laugh. Then I heard that Mr. Abbott was there. I thought, that finishes me."

Her other at-a-distance encounter with Abbott was

during an open-call chorus audition for *Damn Yankees*. That did her no good either. But finally the Eckarts, working with Abbott in preparation for the musical comedy *Once Upon A Mattress*, talked to the big man about Carol. Abbott remembered Carol from the Dutch Treat show and agreed to audition her. Happily for Carol, Abbott had liked the performance which she had thought was a bomb.

"What made it all so unreal was that Jean and Bill had recommended me for the *lead*," Carol said. "Really unreal. The lead!"

It was a March afternoon and Carol was scheduled to audition at four o'clock at the Phoenix Theater on Second Avenue, which is about as far from Broadway as the roof of a five-story loft is from the top of the Empire State Building. The Phoenix is not one of the so-called legitimate Broadway theaters, but Carol didn't mind trying out for an off-Broadway production. If George Abbott—known as Mr. Broadway—was willing to play hookey in the city's backyard to put on a musical comedy, so was Carol willing too. And she remembers just the way it happened:

"I had been given the role of Princess Winifred of Woe. The audition called for dialogue and singing. When I was done, I had no idea what the reaction was."

Carol found out. At six P.M. the phone in her apartment rang. They were calling from the Phoenix to ask if Carol was available for a year. A year?

"I couldn't have been happier," Carol trills as she relives that most happy time. "I'd have committed myself to twelve years. But even if it were to close after the first day, I felt it would be worth it. I'd have paid *them* to let me do it."

At the time, Carol had already made some inroads on the legitimate stage in another area. She had agreed to play in *The Bells Are Ringing*. But that was summer stock and the tour was still some months away. She could always pick up that option if *Mattress* flopped. But, the way Carol felt, there was no way the musical comedy she was to star in could fail.

Not when Richard Rodgers' talented composer daughter, Mary, and lyricist Marshall Barer were doing the songs; not when Joe Layton was staging the musical numbers; and certainly not when George Abbott was there to make certain that the underprivileged prince, a role that went to Jim Maher, was funny, and that the Princess Winifred, whom Carol was to be, was the woebegone pigtailed ruler of a certain desolate swampland with the proper musical-comedy hauteur.

"I learned more about acting from Mr. Abbott than from my three years of dramatics at UCLA," Carol concedes with pride and appreciation. "Mr. Abbott was more wonderful than I'd expected. He taught me so much without ever raising his voice or overworking me. When he said, 'That's good,' it was like a bouquet of roses. Every rehearsal was a ball. But Mr. Abbott would never stand for any hokum or mugging. He wanted us to play it for real, even if it was farce. 'Do it seriously,' he'd say, 'and it's ten times funnier.' "

Abbott never knew how Carol felt about him. At least not until she raved about him later during interviews that popped up in newspapers after the show had opened.

"He wasn't the kind of person you talk to that way," Carol said. "It would have embarrassed him."

On May 11, 1959—just a month short of the expiration of that five-year loan from the wealthy immigrant contractor—Carol Burnett fulfilled her original ambition; she made her stage debut before a capacity opening-night audience in *Once Upon A Mattress*.

The critics gave the play and Miss Burnett rave reviews. Critic Walter Kerr paid tribute to Carol's "restless nose" and "swivel neck" and "cheerfully bandy legs," as well as saluting her for "one of the evening's saucier lyrics," "Happily Ever After." Most importantly, however, the audience too loved the show. They broke up watching Carol clambering aboard a pile of twenty mattresses but finding herself unable to sleep because there was a pea under the bottom one. By evening's end Carol was the town's brightest new musical-comedy star—and she'd continue to enjoy that stature for many more evening and matinee performances.

"Being reviewed by Mr. Kerr and the other critics was a big enough thrill," Carol admits, "but when they said such nice things it was an even bigger thrill."

In the first-night audience were Don Saroyan and Carol's little sister, Chris, who was no longer so little. She was fourteen years old then and had grown taller than her big sister, who at five-feet-seven was no midget herself.

Chris was attending a private school run by the Episcopalian Church in New Jersey because Carol was finally able to afford to give her sister all the better things that she wanted her to have. Carol was even planning to put Chris through college. But it hadn't been so easy at the outset getting Chris into the New Jersey school because when Carol brought her little sister East in 1957 her finances were meager. And Carol had a thing about New York City public schools, which are, of course, tuition-free, but . . .

"That would have been like taking Chris from the frying pan and putting her into the fire," says Carol.

So she went to Martin Goodman and explained that she needed fifteen hundred dollars to start off her kid sister in the school. Goodman went with Carol to the bank and cosigned her loan. Yet putting Chris in school created another problem:

"Chris kept calling up and saying she was homesick. But she finally got adjusted. Chris has always been a wonderful girl. But when I had her with me, I had some other problems. When I was just *Sissy*, everything was fine. When I had to be *Mother*, we had a few fights. But I had to be both just the same."

Handling a growing teenager was one thing. Handling a husband who wasn't on the same wavelength with Carol was something else again. While Carol was in rehearsal for *Once Upon A Mattress*, Don went off to Cuba to work on a film with Beverly Aadland. Carol hadn't wanted him to go, but he was determined to make that big score as an actor.

After he returned he talked about going off to Trinidad on another movie venture. Meanwhile Carol, as a hit on the stage, was more in demand than ever. Before the year was out she had racked up no fewer than ten guest appearances on the Jack Paar's show, she'd been before the cameras of Ed Sullivan's "shew" a total of four times, and had also appeared on *Omnibus* and *Pantomime Quiz*. Add to all that the invitation from Garry Moore to become a regular on his prime-time Tuesday evening slot.

Clearly, Carol Burnett was flying high. But she came in for a bumpy landing around Christmastime.

"Don and I asked what we were doing to each other. Then we said, 'This is it.' We separated. It wasn't one of those screaming 'I hate you' deals. We kept in touch and when we saw each other after that we had more to talk about than we used to have."

It bothered Don to have his wife as the big breadwinner in their household. Carol tells it straight:

"He could have said, 'Okay, my wife's working, so I'll sit on my duff.' He didn't do that. It bothered him that I was making more money and the situation was unnatural."

Sometime after the separation Carol told Pete Martin in an interview for the *Saturday Evening Post*: "Chances are, if I marry again, I'll still make more money than my husband. In this business, if you're in demand, you're overpaid."

Carol's glimpse into the future didn't precisely set her up to claim clairvoyance among her many talents. She would marry again (in fact, Carol had already met him before her separation from Don), but the man would be far from Carol's financial secondary.

But a romance with that man then was the farthest thing

from Carol's mind. For, after all, what woman in her right mind could contemplate romance with a seemingly happily married man with eight children?

5

"An important reason for the success this season of the *Garry Moore Show* on Tuesday nights over the Columbia Broadcasting System network is an exuberant young woman named Carol Burnett. Her work on the weekly television program, in which she has delighted audiences with her impersonations of slightly daffy creatures in a variety of comic predicaments, is only part of her current show business activity . . . ."

That was how John P. Shanley put it in *The New York Times* of March 6, 1960, in a feature story about Miss Burnett. He went on to remind readers that Carol also was still heading the cast of *Once Upon A Mattress.*

By then the play was in its tenth month and drawing standing-room-only crowds. But the audiences were triple the size of the capacity throngs that had packed the Phoenix on opening night and for months afterward. No, they didn't enlarge the Second Avenue theater; *Mattress* was merely moved out of that playhouse to Broadway. And Carol had done it almost singlehandedly.

It all started when the Phoenix's management handed George Abbott an eviction notice because the theater had scheduled *Lysistrata* for the fall season. The news shook up Carol and the others in the cast like an earthquake. Carol still burns over that incident:

"We had pulled the Phoenix out of the red and then

they were kicking up out. It was ridiculous. We were the first show in six years to keep that theater open all summer. So now we were getting evicted."

That's a mild statement compared to Carol's language at the time:

"It's a crime that the Phoenix people didn't have the foresight to get us another house. Why don't they take *Lysistrata* someplace else? It'll probably be a bomb, anyway. Don't tell me about Phoenix policy. Let's face it, they sure do some lousy old plays. They shy away from anything that entertains people."

Carol's actions were even stronger than her words. She had the mattresses piled high during the final act, and right from the stage she climbed atop and appealed to the audience to write letters of protest to the Phoenix management. She also organized the cast's twenty-six members and picketed the theater. Some of their signs read:

WHY CLOSE A HIT?
S.O.S.—SAVE OUR SHOW
WE NEED A HOME

Amazingly, many of the signs weren't being carried by members of the cast; youngsters from the neighborhood had joined the picket line! The reason for that alliance was Carol Burnett.

From the day rehearsals had started at the Phoenix for *Once Upon A Mattress*, Carol took her breaks for a sandwich and soda at the candy store next door. Boris and Sylvia, who owned the shop, were thrilled over "a big TV star coming to our little store." So were the neighborhood kids. Business at Boris and Sylvia's store went up-up-up. Youngsters from blocks away flocked to the store to catch a glimpse of Carol. Many walked over to her and told her how much they loved her.

More boys and girls would wait at the corner to walk her to the stage door. Crowds of young boys vied for the chance to fill her water pitcher with ice. They even saved up their money for weeks and decorated the candy store with garlands of crepe paper, bought a cake, got dressed in their Sunday best, and threw her a party after one Saturday matinee.

Just why that sort of thing happened was obvious—it was that the young generation loved Carol's antics on TV. And perhaps, too, it was as Sylvia from the candy store said:

"She gives them a chance to like her."

But during the picketing a New York columnist suggested that Carol had conned the kids into the picket line with fifty-cent bribes. But that knight of the quill later retracted that suspicion and apologized in print—after Carol had bellowed her outrage to his editor.

Carol's campaign to save *Once Upon A Mattress* aroused so much feeling that the show readily found a new home uptown at the Alvin Theater—on Broadway! Now twice as many theatergoers were able to see the musical comedy at each performance. Yet a time came when *Mattress* was compelled to depart the Alvin, because a previously scheduled show was coming in. So Carol and the cast moved temporarily into the spacious Winter Garden. That was one of Carol Burnett's biggest moments.

"I had the dressing room in the Winter Garden that Rosalind Russell had in *Wonderful Time*, one of the grandest in New York," Carol reminisced. "It had three rooms and a pink bathtub. I loved it because I've always been bath-happy anyway. I was talking about installing a hot plate in the bathroom and living there, while subletting my apartment."

But the Winter Garden also turned out to be only a temporary shelter for *Once Upon A Mattress*. That theater too was committed to let another company use its facilities, so Carol and cast had to get out once more. Abbott then escorted his players into the St. James Theater, which became their residence for the remainder of the show's run.

With her engagement in the play and her weekly spoof spot on Garry Moore's variety hour, Carol worked her way down from a size twelve to an eight.

"It got so that I was sleep-walking in the daytime,"

Carol said. "I became accident-prone, too, because I was so sleepy and didn't know what I was doing. In one short stretch I ripped my thumb, sprained my ankle twice, and my back once. I also cracked my arm and came down with walking pneumonia."

But along the tiring way Carol was gaining maturity, popularity, and an increasingly tighter grip on stardom. Yet at the same time she also harbored a pernicious fear of becoming "typed" as a comedienne. Television, she felt, was doing that to her, but not Broadway. However, both TV and the stage were affording her a feeling of comfort and assurance that she could never find in doing a nightclub act.

"I was fearful of being alone out on a nightclub floor all by myself," Carol admitted. "I don't like playing to people who come there primarily to drink. In TV and on Broadway you're in with fellow players, and you're playing different characters. What's more, you're playing to people who want to be entertained, and who are there for that purpose."

While Carol spoke a great deal about her fear of being slotted in the comedienne's groove, she did not try too strenuously to shake that identification. She seemed to be perfectly content being TV's funny woman, week in, week out. But that didn't stop her from airing her complaints, as she did in an interview in September 1960:

"TV viewers think of me as only one thing. They want me to make them laugh, that's all. Okay, that's what I do, but it's only part of the bit. Broadway gives me the chance to get out there and belt out a song in a serious vein, it lets me pull a few sight gags and funny lines, and be dramatic as well. All around, understand? That's what I meant about TV putting you in that typed groove, that comfortable little rut that's so hard to get out of if you stay there too long."

Looking back over the fifteen years since she uttered those words, what has Carol Burnett done that changed the course of her professional career since 1960?

For the last eight TV seasons Carol Burnett, now in

the forty-first year of her life, has been entrenched in that "typed groove" as America's premiere comedienne and the mistress of her own laugh factory, the *Carol Burnett Show*. Moreover, for the seven years before she became CBS-TV's queen of comedic form in prime time, she pursued a very similar pattern in a variety of other television shows that helped catapult her into her present-day preeminence.

In short, no matter what Carol Burnett says, her fans will not let her be anything other than what they want her to be—a comedienne.

Time and perhaps that "typed groove" which has yielded her great riches seem to have mellowed Carol. Nowadays she doesn't talk with the ardor of old about going back to the legitimate stage. Her tune has changed. (Shortly we'll come to what I think disenchanted and disenfranchised Carol Burnett from the Broadway she had once eagerly sought to conquer—a debacle called *Fade Out-Fade In*.) Today, Carol's view from the top brings a new philosophy:

"I adore doing physical comedy. I love being socked and slapped and thrown out of windows. And doing those screaming roles is better than going to an analyst."

Back in that hectic years of 1960 Carol Burnett didn't only handle her chores in *Once Upon A Mattress* and the *Garry Moore Show*, but many other assignments as well. She managed to squeeze into her tight schedule such additional TV appearances as in *The American Cowboy*, costarring Wally Cox, on CBS; then later that year she flitted over to NBC to take part in a videocast of *No Place Like Home*, sharing equal billing with three other top-ranking movie-TV stars— Rosemary Clooney, Jose Ferrer, and Dick Van Dyke.

When Carol was rehearsing for *No Place Like Home*, her return to the "enemy" NBC studios was cheered by the fellows who pushed the cameras, hung the lights, and swept the studio. The crew on that production hadn't worked with Carol since the *Stanley* series and they were delighted to have her back because she was just plain fun to have around.

What was true then is true today—the CBS crews will tell you that Carol Burnett is a jewel. No grumping around the set, no fits of temperament about the hairdresser, no moody introspective behavior at rehearsals.

A clue of what her effect is like upon the hands who toil on a TV sound stage was offered by a propman:

"I like to work with Carol because her whole personality is up and everyone around her picks up the beat. We love to see her walk in the door."

Her return to NBC for *No Place Like Home* also provided some surprises for the audio men who had worked with Carol on her nonsinging role in *Stanley*. Of course, over at CBS everyone was well acquainted with the strength and range of her voice. But no one there advised the rival network's sound people what to expect in their microphones. Unit manager Sig Bajak was astonished.

"We had to pull our microphones back as far as we did when Ethel Merman sang," Bajak said. "That was the range of Carol's voice. None of us ever expected Carol to have such a big voice. With most people, you put the microphone about eighteen inches away from their mouth" (as they used to do when she sang on the *Paul Winchell Show*) "and let amplification take care of the rest.

"With Carol, we could multiply by three and still know that we were getting terrific sound. The guys looked at each other when she finished the first run-through of that song, "Nobody," and shook their heads. We just couldn't believe it. I guess that's what musical comedy does for you. They have to hear you in the back row—and, brother, they could hear Carol in the back row of the theater next door!"

Bajak made some other observations about Carol that reflect her demeanor in the TV studio:

"One thing you've got to hand to her is that while she doesn't change in her attitude towards people—she's always unassuming and all that stuff—she never stands still professionally. Every minute we didn't have her on

65

stage practicing, she was cornering the choreographer or the choral director or somebody backstage to triple check that she was perfect in everything they wanted her to do. A real pro. Maybe we underestimated her a little when we worked with her before. We knew she was funny, but we had no idea she could sing with such feeling. She's quite a girl."

It has been fifteen years since Carol stood on that NBC stage in New York City, but the memory of her last appearance there has not faded. They still speak fondly of her—and the men who worked with Carol who are still around continue to envy the crews at CBS in New York for having gotten her away from NBC.

The men responsible for getting her on the air love Carol so much that when she finally moved to the Coast and began airing her shows from Television City in Hollywood, half the crew in New York requested transfers so they could continue working with her!

After she completed filming *No Place Like Home* back in November 1960 she found an opportunity to fulfill a commitment with one of her UCLA classmates. Seven years earlier she and Len Weinrib had made a pact at college. Carol remembers what was said:

"We agreed that maybe someday we would work together professionally. A time finally came when we did. It was a big thrill for me."

In the years since Carol and Len had made that pact, Weinrib had gone on to star in the *Billy Barnes Revue* both in Hollywood and in New York. He also had scored heavily as a regular on the *Spike Jones Show*, on CBS. Then, at long last for Len, he was paired with Carol on the *Garry Moore Show*. They were a hilarious combination—just as they'd been at UCLA when they tore the place apart. Weinrib remembered that episode:

"We went into an empty classroom to rehearse. We looked each other over like a pair of fighters, then we tried to prove which one of us was funnier. For a half hour it was bedlam. First Carol pretended to be teaching a class in crazy accents. Then I took to jumping around on

66

the chairs and singing. We finally fell into each other's arms, exhausted, and agreed that it had been a half hour of sheer idiocy."

Judging from her antics on TV, one could say that Carol Burnett has not changed since those zany college days.

In the spring of 1961 Carol Burnett was visited by Charles Collingwood for *Person To Person*. The show, originally introduced by the late Edward R. Murrow, consisted of a very simple format. TV cameras and crew descended on some noted personality's home or apartment and, while electricians, soundmen, and the rest of the gang were making second-hand furniture out of new, Collingwood spoke with the host and took viewers on a guided tour of the digs.

Well, by now Carol had moved out of the dingy West Fifty-fourth Street flat that she had shared with Don Saroyan and gotten herself a plush, $325-a-month terrace apartment on Seventy-second Street near Central Park. When the show was aired on Friday night, June 30, there was one stark switch from the conventional tour, when the celebrity guest showed the rented paintings. Carol showed off her sister, Chris, and their Yorkshire terriers, Bruce (the female) and Fang (the male).

Collingwood also had Carol waving to the construction men working on a building going up alongside her apartment house. Carol had never waved to them before, nor after the program. She hated them. They had been keeping her awake with all the noise they were making.

Well, if Carol Burnett wasn't a celebrity after all she'd done on Garry Moore's show, she certainly was one then for having been on *Person To Person*.

Carol's heightened celebrity status was due for another boost. No sooner had she performed in the last episode of the season on the *Garry Moore Show* than there was talk that she'd soon be doing her own *Carol Burnett Show* for TV. By August 1961 the rumor was full blown.

Carol finally reacted with a "Who me?" She said she had no ambition to take a starring role either in a TV special or series.

"Being a second banana has all the advantages and none of the headaches involved in having your own show," she said defensively. Moreover, Carol pointed out, her contract with Garry Moore for the 1961–62 season had a provision that permitted three absences that could be applied to road tryouts—if the right play came along for her. Carol's enthusiasm for the Broadway stage was still undiminished.

At the moment, however, Carol had other plans. She was preparing for a trip to Europe. And on the following Saturday, August 6, she was off on the *Liberté* on her first Atlantic crossing.

Carol's first stop was England, where she disinterred her Blue Angel routine and the John Foster Dulles ditty for two appearances on Granada-TV's *Chelsea At Nine*. The usually harsh London critics gave Carol gratifying reviews.

Then it was off to France for a bona-fide vacation that Carol played "strictly by ear." When she returned to New York she was summoned by Garry Moore to start rehearsals for the fall season.

"It was an easier schedule then because I didn't have to contend with doing my Princess Winifred bit every night plus Wednesday and Saturday matinees, and rehearsing with Garry during the day every day," Carol said. "Do you know I went from one hundred and twenty one down to one hundred and six in that hectic and insane period? By the end of the season I looked like John Carradine in drag."

But Carol Burnett was still going at full speed, and in all directions. Now she was heading into the teeth of another gale—her own CBS network radio show five evenings a week with Richard Hayes. And she still hadn't abandoned her desire to do another Broadway show.

Why did she let herself be sucked into the vortex of

that passé medium called radio when she had so much else going for her?

"I had never done a radio show before and it's part of show business," Carol explained. "In TV you have all your equipment going for you. A puckish face can help build laughs, get you an audience reaction. Radio has no such built-in advantages. You reach them by voice alone. That was challenging enough for me. Also, I always liked to sing. The framework of the *Garry Moore Show* permitted me little of that, except for brief snatches on the 'Wonderful Year' segment."

With Richard Hayes, Carol performed on the air with what she calls "less-written" scripts, which afforded her opportunities not only to sing the gossamer strains of such composers as Kern, Gershwin, and Schwartz (gentle, non-brassy, modulated melodies not often offered to her when working in broad comic strokes), but she could also chat informally to her heart's content with Dick Hayes on matters that interested them both.

However, the main thrust of her efforts was toward the *Garry Moore Show* that fall season of 1961. She loved working for Garry, and the feeling was mutual. In an interview with Garry back then when I was working for Hearst's *New York Journal-American*, I asked for his evaluation of Carol Burnett. He gushed like an Oklahoma oilwell with praises for Carol. I got enough quotes from him not only to do a piece for my newspaper but also a feature for one of the TV magazines.

When I started research and interviews for this book, I asked Garry whether in the more than dozen years since the vivacious redhead had left his show anything had happened to make him change the view he had of her back in those early days of the sixties.

"Only that I think more of her now," he said. Then I read his quotes from that old interview and asked whether he'd want to change anything.

"Not a word," he responded.

This is what Garry Moore had to say about Carol when his memory of her was freshest:

"The day I saw her I knew she was something. In this business you see them come and go, and I must have seen thousands. I've seen them with and without talent, with and without looks, with and without good figures. But when I saw Carol and she began speaking to me—and later when I auditioned her—I knew that show business had a natural in her.

"It's something you can't quite define, this business of looking at a lineup of beautiful, glamorous girls all dying to be selected. And somehow you point your finger at just one, often without knowing just why. Yet I know why I hired Carol—because she is great. I watch her come on stage. There is something about her—an infectious, a magnetic, dynamic audience-appeal quality that is the true measure of star quality.

"She can smile and the entire set lights up. She has everybody in a state of near-collapse from laughing—and that includes cameramen, sound technicians, engineers, and the whole production staff. Not to mention the cast.

"Her main asset is that she can be enormously funny yet retain her femininity and wholesomeness. She captures her audience by doing what comes naturally for her. And she is always willing to try anything—she never quits learning."

Garry Moore remembers that at the outset with his show Carol Burnett was a stand-up comic whose routines were infectious, hilarious, and tremendously popular with the viewers. But in time, Moore related, Carol realized that that was not her forte.

"She wanted to do more than stand-up stuff," Garry said. "Her comedy sense had become sharper. Basically, it's important to realize she's a sketch comedienne, and my biggest satisfaction was in being able to persuade her that she is not a grotesque girl but someone with a great deal of charm and sex appeal. Above all that, she was in every way a *girl*."

I asked Moore whether Carol was ever given to a display of temperament.

"Temperament?" Garry came back. "Why, Carol

70

doesn't know the meaning of the word. She's a warm, gentle girl, although very outgoing and frank. Certainly, once in a while Carol would tell me what she thought—look at what she told the people at the Phoenix Theater. But lose her head? Never. Sure, she's uninhibited and she's got a free-swinging nature. But that's refreshing and delightful to have around. Carol's a real pro."

To this day Carol is deeply grateful to Garry Moore for all he did for her and for the help he provided in furthering her career.

"I adore Garry and I'll always be indebted to him for the fatherly attitude he took toward me," Carol wants the world to know. "His little words of wisdom, his guidance, the way he instilled confidence in me when things went wrong—they've helped make me the kind of performer I am today. There are few people as fine as Garry in this business. He's one in a million."

During the 1961–'62 season Carol's appearance on the *Garry Moore Show* gained mounting approbation with each passing Tuesday night. Yet an observer sitting through rehearsals couldn't help but wonder how the show, successful as it had been week in and week out, was going to make it on the air at the next telecast. The rehearsals invariably seemed to move in low gear and with little apparent enthusiasm.

"Sure we'd give it the works when we actually did the show on the air," Carol once explained to Pete Martin when she was still working with Garry Moore. "You do get revved up when you face an audience. It makes your adrenalin spurt. It's magic."

In that interview, which appeared in *The Saturday Evening Post*, Carol described working with Moore:

"If Garry has a very funny line in a sketch and he thinks it would be funnier if I said it, he'll give it to me. He doesn't want to be the whole hog. This is one of the secrets of his TV indestructibility. It also shows how carefully he guards my best interests. Moreover, he kind of rations me to the public, and he's right. He doesn't use me to the point where the audience tires of me. I may

71

be on twelve minutes. I may be on less. That's just fine. I'm not a star, and that's the way I want it to be."

More recently Carol told me:

"I don't know where I would be today if it hadn't been for Garry Moore. I owe him so very much."

One of the strongest contributors to Carol's success on the Moore show (aside from Garry) was Durward Kirby, who invariably was a foil for Miss Burnett. Kirby, who had started as an announcer doing commercials, developed into a competent comedian on Garry's show.

The five-foot-seven Garry would warm up his audience before a show by introducing his six-foot-four second banana, saying, "I suppose you all wonder what Durward Kirby is *really* like? The truth is, Dur is not one person. He's three midgets glued together."

When Carol and Kirby put on their skits, they were riots. They did everything from satirizing the National Safety Council to Grimm's Fairy Tales. Not to mention Carol playing a barking seal with her "trainer" Dur.

"Dur and I put on our little sketches that we made during our rehearsal run-throughs on Fridays," Carol recalled. "Our skits didn't last very long, but they broke up the crew and they made the day seem shorter. Our skits were never dirty, but they were a little risqué at times. We couldn't do some on television.

"In one of our sketches, I remember, Dur was a doctor and I was a patient. He wore a white doctor's coat and I had on horn-rimmed glasses and I said, 'Doctor, I have a problem with my bosom.' Dur told me soothingly, 'It's not noticeable.' I said, 'That's my problem.' "

Carol has never forgotten what her acting teacher at UCLA told her back in 1953: "You have a way of taking a risqué line and making it sound like a baby was saying it."

That quality of unsullied innocence has never deserted her, either as a performer or private citizen. She has no veneer. Moreover she takes a terrific pleasure in puncturing other people. This was never truer than when Carol was working on the *Garry Moore Show*. She had found a particular delight in doing her shopping on Fifth Avenue in rehearsal clothes—levis, a sweat shirt, and sneakers.

The fun involved an unbearably elegant saleswoman whose frozen voice announced a handbag was eighty dollars and who plainly suggested, "Young lady, you cannot afford this bag."

Stored away in Carol's head is that delicious memory of the saleslady's face, a look of utter bewilderment and disbelief, when Carol said casually, "Okay, I'll take it."

But sometimes Carol's humor is entirely private:

"Many years ago, when I went to the *April In Paris* Ball in New York, the classiest social event of the spring season, I went magnificently gowned—and wearing sneakers. But no one, not even my escorts, knew."

The 1961–'62 season of the *Garry Moore Show* had hardly gotten underway when a most shocking development occurred. *New York Post* TV columnist Bob Williams broke a story that Carol was playing her last season with Garry. Williams quoted Carol:

"I don't want to be on TV much more. After all, I'm stagestruck. People who advise me say they might someday want me to have my own TV show. I'm not that interested because I'm chicken. I'm interested in making good. So, supposing I'm a hit. How long could the series run? Four seasons? By that time I'd be typed. And if I get typed as a kook, I'll never get to be Ethel Merman, Mary Martin, or Judy Holliday.

"I'd be *Lucy* and *Margie* or somebody, provided I was lucky. The reason I mention those names is because people are always telling me I resemble them in some way or another. They always say I have a little of Mary Martin in me, or a little of Miss Merman, or Miss Holliday. All I want to be is female, funny, and able to belt a song."

Looking back on that interview and on those times, Carol said:

"I felt that way despite everything I owed to Garry. But I had discussed it with him for a long time. And I had told him: 'Garry, even after I'm gone as a regular,

I'll always come back to be on the show whenever you want me.'"

Suddenly it seemed that Carol was trying to cut off all ties with her highly successful show-business involvements. She was leaving Garry Moore's show, and without a plausible explanation of her plans for her TV career and other future work. Then came her decision to leave the nightly musical variety series on CBS radio, after the broadcast of January 24, 1962. The press information department at CBS put out a flyer attributing to Carol the following:

"I am leaving the show with regret. We started it last September 4, and it has been, from the very beginning, one of my most pleasurable activities. But the pressures of other commitments—the *Garry Moore Show*, plus a planned special this year, preparations for nightclub appearances, the possibility of a Broadway musical comedy —all have been piling up. I had never done a regular radio series before, a dream of mine since childhood. I had welcomed the opportunity to do something a little more informal than what I do on television. Also, radio gave me a chance to sing more, which I especially enjoy, particularly with Richard Hayes. The amazing mail and personal reactions I have received from this CBS series have indicated to me the continuing vitality of radio, and this decision was made very reluctantly."

What hogwash! Consider the circumstances and evaluate the picture back in 1962. Carol was going like gangbusters with Garry Moore. She was really rolling along on CBS Radio. Then, suddenly she was leaving Garry and quitting as Richard Hayes' sidekick. Would Carol have tossed over these prestigious assignments if she hadn't known that something better was in the offing?

You can bet she wouldn't have. And the reason she did was because she was being steered; she was being guided by a man who had become her Svengali.

From all my research on Carol Burnett's life and career I have come to the conclusion that this man was the man who urged her, used all of his influence on her, to leave the Moore show and her radio assignment. Because he had promised her much bigger and better things.

He wasn't giving her a line, either. . . .

Before the 1961–'62 TV season ended for the *Garry Moore Show* Carol and Garry received a flock of awards, including TV's coveted Emmy. In addition to being honored as the top musical-variety performer that year, Carol was also singled out as *TV Guide*'s Favorite Female Performer, and that honor will always stand out in her memory.

"Not because I hadn't expected to win it but because one of the telegrams of congratulations was from Bette Davis, whom I'd never met up to that time."

Carol wept like a baby when the award was presented to her on NBC-TV. Those tears were, as she called them, "tears of gratitude." Moreover, since she hadn't thought she had a chance of winning, she had not prepared a speech.

"When you do, you never win," Carol said.

The presentations show hadn't been off the air but a minute when someone rushed over to Carol calling her to the phone. Garry Moore was on the line with his congratulations.

In the next few days Carol was kept busy answering the phone in her apartment and at the studio as a stream of felicitations poured in. Pretty soon Carol grew weary of the kudos. Only the previous January she had taken bows for another signal honor—Outstanding Television Personality of 1961—from the Headliners' Club in Austin. Carol flew to her native state and received that award from Texas Governor Price Daniel before seventeen hundred persons at a dinner in Austin Memorial Auditorium. Daniel substituted for Vice-President Lyndon B. Johnson, who had been detained in Washington by the postponement of the Project Mercury launching. The award read, in part:

"For her beautiful and delightful contributions of laughter and human warmth to a world filled with tension and fear. For her enchanting modesty and insistence on sharing with others the plaudits of critics and audiences. For remaining a real, down-to-earth person under the pressures of stardom. For giving the Lone Star State another star of which to be proud, and for such a blending of talent and personality that all who know her are pleased to say, 'We love that girl.' "

Later, Carol received still another honor in Austin. At a reception given by the governor in the Executive Mansion she received a Texas goodwill ambassadorship.

Back in New York not many days after the Emmy presentations Carol got a call from a producer aware of her fervor to do another Broadway show. He offered her the lead in the long-planned, much-discussed story of Fanny Brice. Carol's ears perked up. She listened. She was very interested. She then met the producer. They talked about it. Finally—Carol turned the offer down!

"Fanny Brice was a wonderful entertainer but she had a Bronx or New York type of humor, which isn't my type," Carol said. "I'm from the West Coast and my speech has a kind of twang. It would have been an awful problem to get rid of that."

Carol's departure from the *Garry Moore Show* had hardly been announced than an undercurrent of rumors started all at once. . . .

Columnists began hinting that Carol was leaving because she was in love with somebody in the show but that marriage was impossible because he had a wife and a big brood. Naturally, that turned the spotlight on the only person who fit the portrait of a profligate papa—Joseph H. Hamilton, the handsome producer-director of the *Garry Moore Show*. With eight children—five girls and three boys, ranging in age from thirteen to a year and a half—Hamilton had to be the man, everyone reasoned.

But the denials cascaded from the CBS studios like the waters over Niagara. Press agents worked overtime trying to dike the rumors. When Carol was reached finally, she responded, "Romance? I'm too busy for it—unfortunately."

That only made the rumor-mongers search out other candidates who might be Carol's love. One of those was press agent Johnny Friedkin, whom Carol had dated now and then. Another was actor Richard Chamberlain, the star of the *Dr. Kildare* TV series.

But none of the enterprising scriveners could make much of a case out of Chamberlain, Friedkin, or Hamilton —at least, not yet. . . .

Meanwhile, an event of considerable significance occurred just before Carol's stint as a regular had run out on the *Garry Moore Show*. She fulfilled one of her long-held ambitions: She sent plane fare to her grandmother, Mrs. Mae White, so that she could come to see her granddaughter perform in person.

"When Nanny came to the studio," Carol laughed, "she marched in like she owned CBS. She wanted to sit down in front. An usher told her she couldn't. She said, 'But I'm Carol Burnett's grandmother.' The usher said, 'Well, bully for you!' She thought he was congratulating her."

6

Christine Burnett was watching her sister, Carol, performing in one of her last regular appearances on the *Garry Moore Show*. Chris was going on eighteen, and graduation from the private school she was attending in Mendham, New Jersey, was just weeks away. Carol's mobile features and slapstick style, which had kept TV fans howling week after week during her long tenure on Moore's show, had also provided Chris with that same delightful escape each Tuesday night when she'd sit with a bunch of the girls in front of the TV set in the lounge at school.

On that particular night in the spring of 1962 Carol was doing a skit with Garry in which she was portraying a champagne-hungover Cinderella the morning after the grand ball. The scene went like this:

GARRY: How did you enjoy the ball?

CAROL: *Must* you shout?

GARRY: How did you get to the ball?

CAROL: Things are a little hazy . . . there was a fairy godmother . . . a pumpkin, mice . . . oh, boy, never again!

GARRY: Did you lose a shoe?

CAROL: I wouldn't be at all surprised.

Of course the hangover was a put-on, part of the act. But to Chris there was something about the way Carol looked that wasn't right. Her face seemed drawn. The eyes were tired. Chris went to her room and penned a note to Carol—a note that Carol has cherished all the days since.

"Usually Chris would write me a three-sentence note asking for money, but this letter brought tears to my eyes," Carol said. The message:

Dear Sissy:
I miss you very much. It just killed me to see you looking so thin. I know that you are working very hard, but money can't buy good health. So please take better care of yourself. You can't live on sweet rolls and coffee.

I love you,
Chris

A few weeks later Chris graduated and after the exercises she returned with Carol to New York for summer vacation. In the fall Carol was to keep her promise to send her "baby" sister to college. But for the summer Chris would stay with Carol, who planned to take a long rest and do some of the things the two sisters loved— water ski, swim, and bowl.

But their plans didn't work out. Carol had agreed earlier to do a summer tour of several cities with Julie Andrews, with whom she had recently completed taping a special at Carnegie Hall. Carol, who had appeared with Miss Andrews on the *Garry Moore Show* a year earlier, was thrilled with the idea of going on the road with Julie —especially after their classic performance at Carnegie Hall. It was called *Julie and Carol at Carnegie Hall* and was filmed before a black-tie audience on the night of March 5.

Although CBS did not put it on the air until the night of June 11, there'd been no doubt that Carol and Julie were a hit again working together. For the capacity audience in Carnegie Hall had gone ape over the girls and their bright, fresh, clever material—especially their "Nausiev Dancers" number, satirizing the Soviet dance groups, and the "Pratt Family," a spoof of the Trapp Family in *Sound of Music.*

The writing credits belonged to Mike Nichols and an old friend, Ken Welch, who had prepared Carol's seven-minute audition for Garry Moore and had since written a great deal of material for her. Although the girls had the lusty assistance of a twenty-man chorus as they slam-banged their way through the big production numbers, the show was basically a two-woman performance.

Carol and Julie undertook a medley of musical comedy songs which turned into a competition between them; Carol sang Julie's number, "Wouldn't It Be Loverly," in her own raucous way, and Julie took Carol's "I'm Just A Girl Who Can't Say No" and rendered it in her dainty, dignified style.

Thus it seemed to Garry Moore's producer-director, Joe Hamilton, that the success of Carol and Julie in their TV special should be carried on the boards of the straw-hat circuit. The girls agreed. But then the unexpected happened: Julie Andrews became pregnant. Carol was de-lighted. Now she could have the summer off and enjoy the sports and outdoor life that she and Chris liked so much.

"But the *vacation* turned out to be taking Chris along with me on tour," Carol groaned.

Joe Hamilton convinced Carol not to back out of the commitment to do the summer tour.

"Do it without Julie," he told her.

And since he had been directing her on the Moore show—and guiding her career in other ways as well—what an easy thing it would be for him to fashion the *Carol Burnett Show* for the road.

Carol let Joe talk her into it. By then Carol had been giving her ear to Joe more and more—and people were buzzing about it. Folks weren't merely whispering about their professional relationship but the growing rapport that was surfacing, a bit obviously, in their private lives.

Joe had recently separated from his wife, Gloria, and

80

moved into a bachelor apartment in Manhattan. Since that time—early January 1962—Carol and Joe had been dating, but very discreetly. Only a few intimate friends knew that Carol and Joe's professional relationship had developed into love—but those few suspected that it was very serious. As one friend put it:

"Those two could have been in two different parts of a crowded room and you could tell everything just by the way they looked at each other. They were as proper in their behavior as could be, but they might as well have sent up rockets saying, 'We love each other.'"

Carol was even dropping little hints that her next husband would be somebody like Hamilton and not Saroyan, whom she had not yet divorced. As early as June 1962 Carol was saying:

"Of course I want to remarry. But he would have to be someone in our business who understands the problems. He won't be a performer. Too much ego involved. That's what happened to Don and me."

Many observers were crediting Hamilton for boosting Carol to her lofty pinnacle in show business, saying that it was his encouragement and imagination as well as his influence on Garry Moore that lifted Carol to stardom. There's no doubt that Hamilton helped her rise, but chances are that Carol Burnett, because she has so much talent, would still have made it on her own. And there's no better argument to back up that claim than the fact that today—more than a dozen years later—she is at the top of her class in comedy and entertainment.

In 1962, when the rumors of their romance began hitting the newspapers, Hamilton was constrained to set the record straight about Carol:

"She really doesn't know how important she is. I tell her, and she breaks records everywhere she goes and gets standing ovations and has millions of fans, and she's still a little timid about audiences. In a way, I think that's rather wonderful, and I hope she keeps that attitude for a while. It's pretty refreshing in this business, don't you think?"

Yes, indeed. And it was apparent that summer that Carol Burnett's star was still in the ascendancy. Joined by the comedy team of Marty Allen and Steve Rossi, Carol's tour brought in banner grosses—$116,748 just in one week in Pittsburgh, for example. But before she was back in New York, dozens of offers were pouring in for Carol—offers to play nightclubs, to star in Broadway musical comedies, and even movies. Carol Burnett was being besieged.

She agreed to work again with Bob Banner Associates, who had staged *Julie and Carol at Carnegie Hall* and had guided her road tour with Hamilton. Now Carol was to star in a ninety-minute musical comedy, *Calamity Jane*, as a CBS-TV special that would be aired in the fall. The role of the rootin' tootin' Jane was familiar to Carol because she had played it in the summer of 1961 at the Starlight Theater in Kansas City during the between-seasons break in the *Garry Moore Show*, after she had returned from her trip abroad.

Carol also accepted a fall booking at New York's famed Persian Room, and she agreed to read the script for a Paramount Pictures comedy, *Who's Been Sleeping In My Bed?*

As if these offers and commitments weren't enough of a challenge, Carol leaped at the opportunity to do another musical comedy on Broadway, a show suggested by Nina Farewell's 1953 book, *The Unfair Sex*. But that production was not going to interfere with Carol's other obligations, for it was programmed as an early entry for the 1963-'64 season, more than a year away.

Meanwhile, those friends of Carol's who were aware of her romance with Joe Hamilton got a big belly laugh from a story out of Hollywood that was headlined in *The New York World-Telegram & Sun*: CAROL BURNETT CONFESSES A CRUSH ON DR. KILDARE

Written in all seriousness, the story professed:

"The most unlikely romantic development of the year is that Carol Burnett of the Garry Moore TV show has a wild crush on video's Dr. Kildare, Richard Chamberlain.

"It started with Miss Burnett three thousand miles away in New York, merely one of the many young maidens whose hearts may have been set aflutter by the handsome actor.

"There were several drawbacks to a romance. For one thing, they had never met, and Chamberlain had no idea of the palpitations he was causing the comedienne-singer.

"For another thing, they work for rival TV networks— she for CBS, he for NBC."

We grant that when two people have not met or when one doesn't know the other cares for him it presents quite a drawback to romance. But that was the first time in journalistic history that employment on rival networks was advanced as a deterrent to love.

That reason has never been used since. Once is enough.

To top it off, the story told of how it meant nothing to Carol that Dick Chamberlain worked for the enemy —she was determined to meet him. It happened, the narrative went on, when Carol had spirited herself to Hollywood one weekend in the fall of 1961 to star in a segment of *Twilight Zone.*

"Her opportunity came when she found that *Twilight Zone* and *Dr. Kildare* were being shot at the same studio, MGM," the story went on.

Then Carol was quoted:

"I bumped into him one day—accidentally, you understand. I almost attacked him."

The writer said that Carol explained her strategy to him at the MGM commissary "as she downed a lunch of Swiss meat balls, tapioca pudding, and other assorted delicacies." Then:

"But Miss Burnett's conversation became somewhat undone as discussion of business was obscured at moments by visions of Cupid and the physical sight of Chamberlain, who was also eating lunch—on the other side of the dining room."

To stress how "undone" Carol became during the interview, the writer purported that this exchange took place:

Q. Miss Burnett, is this your first straight acting part?

83

A. Yes . . . you know, I said I'd never fall in love with an actor, but he's sort of a doctor, isn't he? I've been trying all morning to get a hangnail.

Q. Have you ever had any pin-up pictures?

A. Yeah . . . of Dick Chamberlain.

Q. That's not what I mean.

A. It's what I mean.

When the story broke Carol was lunching with Joe Hamilton at Lindy's. She almost choked on her eggs benedict when one of the waiters came over to the table and showed them the newspaper. They were greatly amused by the story. Indeed, delighted. For they had been doing their darnedest to keep their romance under wraps.

The interview Carol gave in the MGM commissary was one of the foils she employed to throw off suspicion about her and Hamilton. The wonder of it all was that the writer was guillible enough to believe Carol's put-on, and his newspaper so naive as to print it.

Across town, however, the *World-Telegram*'s rival *Journal-American* assigned its ace columnist Dorothy Kilgallen, the "Voice of Broadway," to find out if Carol and Chamberlain were really an item. Since Dorothy had all the ins at CBS-TV, where she was by then a veteran on *What's My Line*, the matter of searching out the truth was a breeze. She soon came up with a declaimer that made Carol Burnett and Joe Hamilton squirm.

"Carol and Richard are about as much in love as Martha Raye and Rock Hudson," wrote Miss Kilgallen. "They're both pleasant people, and there's no reason why they shouldn't see each other—but Carol's real sweetie is a handsome television executive, separated from his wife and many children, just waiting for the popular comedienne to get her divorce."

That account had more or less taken a tooth from the ancient saw about "where there's smoke, there's fire." For, as a matter of fact, by the time Miss Kilgallen's piece appeared, Carol had carried her diversionary tactics to such lengths as to actually go out on dates with Richard Chamberlain!

That happened when the summer circuit of the *Carol Burnett Show* wended its way into the Sands Hotel in Las Vegas. That stopover was agreed to by Carol for a very personal reason—to establish Nevada residency so that she could divorce Don Saroyan.

But in those late days of summer no one suspected the real purpose of Carol's extended stay at the Sands. Chris was with her and the reasoning was that big sister was letting little sister have her last fling before putting her nose to the educational grindstone at Moravian College in Bethlehem, Pennsylvania, where she was to begin her freshman semester in the fall.

It was during this hiatus in Vegas that Carol went out with Chamberlain and caused Dorothy Kilgallen's line about "there's no reason why they shouldn't see each other . . ." As a matter of fact, Carol also dated Raymond Burr in Vegas, which gave the legal profession an equal footing with the medical fraternity in Carol's affections.

But if that piece by Dorothy had shaken up Carol and Joe when it appeared on August 29, imagine what Miss Kilgallen's eight-column, page-one banner headline story in the *Journal-American* on August 31 did to them: CAROL BURNETT IS 'IN LOVE WITH A WONDERFUL GUY'

Of course, it couldn't have been that much of a stunner either to Carol or Joe, for Dorothy had already spoken to both of them. No one could say that they didn't suspect it was coming. But few others did and the story created seismic shocks everywhere.

"America's favorite comedienne, Carol Burnett, is in love with a wonderful guy, and they expect to be married 'when everything is straightened out,'" Miss Kilgallen started out. "The lucky fellow is Joseph H. Hamilton. . . ."

Then Miss Kilgallen quoted what Carol had told her over the phone from the Sands:

"I'm madly in love with him."

And what Joe told Dorothy in New York:

"The feeling is mutual."

There it was. The romance that Carol Burnett and Joe Hamilton had tried to keep under wraps had finally erupted like a volcano. The wire services picked up the story and by late afternoon *The Las Vegas Sun* had it emblazoned on its front page. When the newspaper was brought to Carol's suite, tears came to her eyes as she read the story.

"I hope they will understand. . . ."

The words were uttered by Carol to Chris in their Sands suite. Carol's great concern then was what the public reaction would be. Carol was particularly disturbed by this key paragraph:

"He" (Hamilton) "approached his wife, the former Gloria Hartley, about a divorce, and hoped it would not be too long before they could come to an amicable agreement that would make it possible for him to marry Carol. *The Hamiltons have eight children—five girls and three boys, ranging in age from thirteen to a year and a half.*"

The underscoring is ours, to emphasize what was in Carol's mind. She was terrified that unless people understood how she and Joe had become involved, she might be accused of being a homewrecker.

And that's exactly what Joe Hamilton's wife told me that Carol was. . . .

7

"Carol Burnett has my Joe. I suppose that's what she wanted . . . and I hope she's happy."

Gloria Hartley Hamilton's voice broke as she talked with me about the divorce and her husband's immediate remarriage to Carol Burnett. But that's getting ahead of the story. . . .

LAS VEGAS, Nev. Sept. 25 (AP)—The seven-year marriage of Carol Burnett, the comedienne, and Don Saroyan, an actor, ended today in District Court. Miss Burnett charged extreme mental cruelty. The couple, who had no children, separated in 1959. A sealed property settlement was reached.

That's all the attention that Carol's divorce from Don received even after all the hullabaloo raised only three weeks earlier by the news of Miss Burnett's romance with Joe Hamilton. It was to be eight months more before Carol and Joe embarked on their connubial excursion.

But before we get to that, and to the first Mrs. Hamilton's reactions to Joe and Carol, let's not neglect the progress of Carol's career. We dug up a handout issued by the CBS Television Network at 485 Madison Avenue in New York back in January 1963:

"For vivacious Carol Burnett, 1962 proved to be a

truly 'wonderful year,' with her career zooming to new heights. The memorable twelve months were highlighted by the signing in August of an exclusive, long-term contract with the CBS Television Network. It calls for the redheaded comedienne to star in a number of specials—the first, *An Evening With Carol Burnett*, to be broadcast Sunday, February 24, 1963, on the CBS Television Network. Under terms of the pact, she will also be a guest on regularly scheduled programs. . . ."

The CBS release neglected a few very significant details, such as the salary Carol was to get—a hundred thousand dollars a year for ten years, which made the pact a million-dollar deal. Nor did it mention Joe Hamilton's influence and efforts in laying the groundwork for the contract. And nothing was said about Hubbell Robinson, senior vice-president in charge of network TV programs, getting Carol as a guest on four Garry Moore shows during the 1962–'63 season. And not a word was breathed in the release about Robinson's plans to have Carol do a regular weekly series, a series that Miss Burnett was offered by the rival NBC-TV network and which she turned down.

Carol had agreed to do the series but when she came to terms with CBS she was certain that she couldn't do it for the 1962–'63 season. Robinson had no objection to that, but he let Carol know that CBS stood ready to proceed with the show "if you should change your mind."

Carol couldn't even consider the series for the 1962–'63 season because she had agreed to do *Who's Been Sleeping In My Bed*? for Paramount and, in addition, had many other engagements, including a CBS-TV show with Jack Benny in the fall of 1962.

"How many times do I have to tell you I'm Jane *you* Tarzan!"

That was the line which Carol repeated over and over during her Tarzan skit with Benny in Hiawatha wig and leopard-skin leotard, which was aired shortly before Thanksgiving of 1962. Benny, it is said, sulked for weeks and weeks after Carol's guest appearance on the show. The salary he had to pay her made him so sad.

There's a degree of ambivalence in Carol Burnett that shows up in her interviews. Take, for example, her recollections of her childhood. Was she a *popular* kid in school or was she *miserable*? In her 1961 interview with Pete Martin, Carol said:

"Not long ago I was being interviewed by a beady-eyed little man who made me feel as if I were under analysis. He asked, 'Why do you do comedy? Is it because you *want* to have people love you? Is it because you suffer a deep sense of insecurity from being cuffed around as a kid?' I told him, 'Everyone wants to be loved. That's normal. But as a child I never had to clown to make people like me.' Not that I ever felt particularly gorgeous, but I was a good athlete in school. I had a lot of friends. I wasn't homely, nor was I terribly attractive. I was just average."

Eight years later, in mid-1969, Carol Burnett had yet another recollection of her youth. She told Tom Burke, of *The New York Times*:

"God, I was a miserable teenager. I admit that I get a kick out of seeing people now whom I was scared of in high school, because they were so popular or pretty. But you can't get hung up on gloating. Like, there were these two sisters in my class who were on the cover of *Life* for being the most beautiful teenagers in California. I'd pass them in the halls and they'd suck in their cheeks. I'd go home and try to wave my hair like theirs and I'd look like King Kong.

"Okay, a week ago Joe" (Hamilton, who by that time was Carol's husband) "and I were having dinner with a bachelor friend with his date—the prettiest of the two sisters. I said to myself, 'Thank you, God, there is retribution. I've waited for this!' Well, I wait a little longer, until she's into the menu—she's still beautiful, still sucks in the cheeks—when I say, 'Uh, you may not remember, Madeline, but we went all through high school together.'

"Dead silence. She finally says, very bored, 'Oh, really? Do you want to see the menu, Carol?' Shot down!

She couldn't have cared less! Now that was a humbling experience."

Let's return to that late August day of 1962 after Dorothy Kilgallen broke the story of Carol being in love with "a wonderful guy."

My city editor on *The Journal-American* had asked Miss Kilgallen to try for a *follow* on the story for the next day's editions. He wanted Dorothy to interview Carol by phone for some "intimate quotes," as he described the assignment. But Dorothy wasn't fascinated by the idea. She had enough to do gathering material for her daily syndicated column. She had given the *J-A* the beat on the story. Now, Dorothy felt, some lower-echelon staffer ought to do that legwork, not she. So the assignment was given to me. I reached Carol at the Sands. She was locked in her suite with Chris. They had just read the story in *The Las Vegas Sun.*

"I was wondering what the reaction would be," Carol told me. "I didn't want to say anything, but I don't see how we can hide something like this. Now that the cat is out of the bag, I guess it's just as well."

I asked Carol if she and Joe had set a wedding date.

"Too soon to tell," Carol told me. "I'm here in Las Vegas on tour, but I'm taking advantage of my Nevada residence to file for divorce. It's all very friendly. Don understands that it has to be this way. We separated the best of friends. Don's in San Diego working as a resident producer and director for a musical theater. He's doing what he really wants, and it's only since we parted that he has begun to find himself. It was the best way."

Carol also spoke about her plans for the immediate future:

"After the divorce I'm coming back to New York. I have a busy schedule. That may even include a trip to London to do a show and visit friends like Julie Andrews and her husband. I may stay through Christmas into early next year. I hope to have Chris come there during her school holidays. Then we'll come back together in early January."

Then I got through to Joe Hamilton, who told me:

"The separation from my wife was amicable. I have discussed divorce with her and she is willing to go through with it. We have come to an arrangement. Things will have to be worked out. It'll take a little time."

And what was Garry Moore's reaction to the story of Carol and Joe's love—now that the story was out in the open?

"Carol and Joe," Garry said to me, "are wonderful people. They work together like no two people I know. They deserve all the happiness in the world."

Carol Burnett and Joe Hamilton headed for their happiness on May 4, 1963—a Saturday. It happened not many weeks after Carol had been dunked in a pool in her bridesmaid's outfit. But that was before the cameras in Hollywood, where Carol had launched her movie career and was doing a scene from *Who's Been Sleeping In My Bed*? After she was dunked in the pool, Marty Allen, of Allen & Rossi, watched Carol come out of the pool sopping wet. Marty, who had appeared with Carol the previous summer on tour, proved helpful—he pushed her back into the water.

After the scene for the movie was finished, Carol was ready to take the plunge with Joe. It turned out to be a sticky, frenetic dash into the matrimonial sweepstakes.

When Carol and Joe—they had first flown to New York to pick up Chris, who had the weekend off from Moravian College—jetted to Mexico, they had no idea that civil marriage on a Saturday is virtually impossible south of the border. The courts are closed over the weekend, just as in the USA. Moreover, even Joe's divorce from Gloria had not yet been obtained.

But Hamilton had worked things out with his West Coast attorney, Simon Taub, so that when he and Carol got to Juarez, at least the divorce proceedings could be adjudicated. Under Mexican law only one party in the divorce is required to be present. The other may be represented by counsel, power of attorney, or, in the absence of either, can be notified by writ, in which case the divorce is held up until the paper is served.

In the Hamiltons' case, Gloria was doing the divorcing —not Joe, as it was widely believed at the time.

"Joe didn't divorce me. I got the divorce. I'd like to make that clear. . . ."

The grounds for the divorce, in Mexican terminology: "Incompatability of temperament." No sooner had Joe gotten his divorce than he and Carol headed for the chambers of Judge Baltazar Aquire, who had to be petitioned to come from his home on that Saturday when court was not in session. After the ceremony Chris, who'd served as witness and maid-of-honor, flew back to Pennsylvania and Carol and Joe flew to Los Angeles. They were headed on a Hawaiian honeymoon.

When the newlyweds put down at the airport in Los Angeles to change planes they were spotted by a photographer. He asked if she was Carol Burnett. The reply:

"No, I am now Mrs. Hamilton."

Incidentally, the Associated Press wire story, undoubtedly picked up from the Los Angeles newspapers, listed Carol's age as twenty-eight, which shows with what gullibility supposedly infallible newspaper editors fall for press agents' "facts."

At least they had Joe Hamilton's right age—thirty-seven.

As the AP teletype clacked out the first paragraphs of the divorce-and-remarriage saga my city editor assigned me to get a "reaction story" from Gloria Hamilton.

I drove to her home in the fashionable suburb of Scarsdale, just north of New York City—a fifteen-room home that was really a mansion, a home that Joe had bought for Gloria and the children only the previous September.

"Please don't ask me how I feel about Carol," Mrs. Hamilton said to me. "It wouldn't be right to say anything. How can I tell you how I feel after this—I'm hurt one day, angry the next. My feelings change from day to day. . . ."

I was instantly impressed by her appearance. She was a pretty and petite ninety-pound blonde, elegantly trim and stylish and with a stark resemblance to Marilyn Monroe. She'd been Joe's wife for fifteen years.

"Joe and I were childhood sweethearts," Mrs. Hamilton said after I had broken the ice with her. "We lived very near each other. I was raised with his whole family. I can't remember a time when he wasn't 'my Joe.' There were the high school dances, movies, sodas . . . We were married right out of high school. We were so happy. I gave him eight children—and now this has happened. . . ."

Until my interview with Gloria, the word around town was that she and Joe had been experiencing "irreconcilable differences" for quite a while, and that was why they had separated. But in talking with the ex-Mrs. Hamilton, a new light was cast on those "irreconcilable differences."

"The stories about Carol and Joe started a long time ago," Gloria said. "Then the columnists began dropping little hints in their writings. No names—but I knew who they meant. It was a very unpleasant thing. I tried to keep it from the family—Joe's family. Then Joe came to me and said he wanted a divorce. Of course I refused. But it didn't end there. He kept asking again and again.

"For several months that's all I heard. "Gloria, I want a divorce.' I couldn't understand it. I'm not a Catholic, but Joe is. I raised the children to believe in the Church—in the Catholic faith. His faith. And then this happens—the very thing that the Catholic Church forbids: divorce."

Gloria's feelings were shared by every member of Joe Hamilton's immediate family. Almost as one they rose in rebellion against Joe when it became known that he had stolen off to Juarez to get his divorce and marry Carol. Kip Hamilton Geisel, Joe's sister, and her mother, Mrs. Joseph H. Hamilton, rushed to Gloria's side when they learned what was happening.

They came to console Gloria and do what they could to comfort the children. Kip, whose husband, David, was working with Joe on the *Garry Moore Show*, was as outspokenly critical of Carol as Gloria was.

"I can never accept Carol as my sister-in-law," Kip told me. "I simply refuse to see Carol. She's very nice and she's talented. She's always been wonderful to me. But I have a sister-in-law in Gloria, a sister couldn't be closer. It would be very confusing if we had to divide our loyalty and love. If Carol's as sensitive as I think, she'll be hurt. But I'd rather hurt her than Gloria."

My big question to Gloria about their eight children scraped on an open wound. I said it had been reported that Joe had discussed the divorce with those of the children who were old enough to understand.

"No, Joe never had the courage even to discuss this thing with the children," Gloria said, her voice choking. "Never once at all. The older children read about it in the newspapers—and about his remarriage. Fortunately, I had prepared them beforehand.

"When Joe and I began to discuss the divorce finally, I got the children together and told them that their father wouldn't be living with us anymore. 'You'll understand better when you're older,' I told them—but I wonder if they will. I had to tell them beforehand. It was cruel enough for them to hear reports on TV and to read about everything in the newspapers without trying to prepare them for the shock."

Gloria's words were drowned out as emotion gripped her. "When did you finally give Joe the okay to get the divorce?" I asked after Gloria had composed herself.

"Joe didn't divorce me," Gloria said. "I got the divorce. I'd like to make that clear. I was the complainant in the case. I made the decision. I got the divorce. It wasn't necessary for me to go to Juarez because I was represented there by my attorney, Arnold Krakower. He'd have to tell you the grounds—I really don't know. I wasn't interested in the legal machinery. All I wanted finally was to be rid of all this trouble. I made the decision. But not necessarily to free my husband so he could marry Carol Burnett, or anyone else for that matter. I simply felt I had had enough of marriage to Joe. It's been very difficult. This thing had gone on so long."

Gloria was very depressed by now. She tightened her jaw and drew her lips together before speaking again.

"From my own experience, I can tell you . . . the wife isn't always the last to know. There comes a point—and I finally reached it—when it becomes necessary to take steps to build a new life for yourself. As a woman married to Joe Hamilton, I realized I could never do that. Now I am married no longer and I'm free to plan."

With that opening, I asked Gloria if there was anyone else in her life.

"I wish I could say there was," she replied. "I haven't had a chance to meet anyone really. I've stuck so close to the children in the last year, trying to protect them from what finally happened, that my interests have been very limited. Now . . . now that it's over, it becomes a problem of my emotional survival. Yet I've learned a lot over the past year.

"And the most important lesson I've been taught is that you do recover—no matter how badly you're hurt. Time cures a lot of things. That's why I decided to go whole way and end my marriage completely. *That was why I got the divorce.*"

Joe's sister, Kip, had told me in a separate interview at the house, "Gloria, of course, still loves my brother. She'll always love him. . . ."

I asked Gloria about that:

"What my sister-in-law says is her business," she declared. "But the statement directly concerns me. Even if I did still love Joe, I wouldn't want anyone else to volunteer it. But the fact is that I am completely indifferent to Joe . . . to Carol . . . and to both of them as husband and wife."

Publicist Jim Eddy, of MacFadden-Eddy—Carol's press agents—had tried to paint a bright picture for Joe's side, since that was the side that was buttering his bread. So Eddy let it be known that Joe Hamilton was to have the children every weekend, holiday vacations such as Easter

95

and Thanksgiving, and all other holidays, as well as one month during the summer. Hamilton was supposed to have "voluntarily waived any right to have the children with him at Christmas."

Those terms, if one could believe Carol's publicist, would have allowed Gloria very little time with the children. So I asked her about the purported arrangement.

"I have complete custody," Gloria said emphatically. "But I'll say this about it—he has reasonable visitation rights, of course."

Gloria also indicated that the terms I recited from the reports were "unrealistic and meaningless." Her account of Hamilton's recent past history with the children indicated that even while still married to Gloria he saw them only at infrequent intervals—and he could not be expected to give them more attention now that he was married to Carol.

However, future events would prove that Joe Hamilton was to turn into more of a full-time father with some of the older children than we were led to believe he had been before the divorce. But during my interview with Gloria, the assessment of Joe as a father was not favorable.

"The last time Joe saw the children was several weeks ago— and then it was only for a minute," Gloria said. "His mother was there, too. If he had such a great interest in the children, he had a chance to tell them himself about the divorce and his plan to remarry. The children knew everything by that time—but he never brought it up, never mentioned anything to them. I have to laugh at these stories that Joe told the children everything himself. He never did. I said he had no courage—and I meant it."

Joe and Carol held to the hope that the children would spend a lot of time with them. Although right after their wedding they lived in her large apartment on Seventy-second Street, they were planning to find a house in Connecticut that fall. Then, they said, they would bring the kids out for weekends and the other times that Joe had rights to have them.

Above: Carol Burnett (right) age 8, with her cousin Janice Vance age 9. Behind Carol is her grandmother Mrs. Mae White, and her aunt, Janice's mother, Mrs. Eudora Vance. *Below:* A picture of Carol in her senior year at Joseph Le Coute Junior High School, Hollywood, California.

Carol on *The Garry Moore Show,* pushed, pulled, choked and generally victimized by the comic pranks of Garry Moore and Durward Kirby.

Some more memorable moments from *The Garry Moore Show* with Garry Moore and Durward Kirby. *Center right:* Carol as Charlie Chaplin.

Right: Carol about to be hit by water.

On the set of film "Who's Been Sleeping In My Bed?" *Opposite right:* With director Daniel Mann.

Right: The water finds its target.

Opposite top: "Shy" — So sings Carol when she makes her first entrance starring as Princess Winnifred in the television adaptation of the off Broadway musical *"Once Upon A Mattress"* which sky-rocketed Carol into stardom. *Opposite center:* With co-star Joe Bova. *Opposite bottom and below:* Scenes from the off Broadway production.

Friedman-Abeles

At three weeks old Erin Kate makes her first appearance in front of a camera in the arms of her mother.

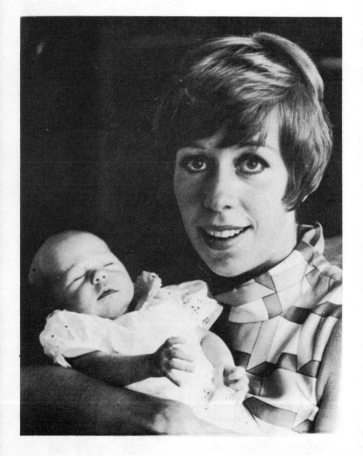

Right: Soaked.

Mr. and Mrs. Joseph Hamilton.

L. A. Airport Photography

Right: Shaking off the water.

Opposite: Carol guest stars on "The Jim Nabors Hour." Lucille Ball and Carol are two of the three clowns in the special "Carol+2." With Jerry Lewis in a comedy sketch. *Below:* Julie Andrews and Carol satirize Russian dancers touring this country, in one of the highlights of "Julie and Carol at Carnegie Hall."

Opposite: Carol and Gwen Verdon team up in a song and dance number, "Come As You Are," on *The Garry Moore Show.* Carol and her guest Robert Preston zip through a fast production number in "Carol and Company," an hour - long special *Opposite bottom:* Carol clowns with Bob Newhart on "The Entertainers." *Below:* Carol with look-alike Vicki Lawrence. Harvey Korman in costume on "The Carol Burnett Show."

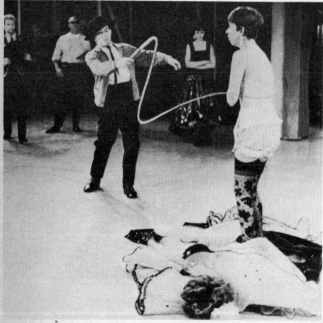

Carol in a "whip-tease" scene for her show has hat (top) and then most of clothes stripped by strokes of whip-lashing dancer. Carol turned thumbs down on double for scene.

Most of the children had met Carol at the CBS-TV studios in New York when they went to see their father and to watch the *Garry Moore Show* rehearsals and tapings. But Kip wasn't certain how the children would feel toward Carol now that she was their father's new wife. Kip told me:

"They had met Carol before any divorce talk. They were impressed with her and thought she was very talented —but that's all."

Then, with derision in her voice, Kip added:

"They already have a mother, you know—and she's a very good one."

But it was Gloria Hartley Hamilton who gave me the strongest statement:

"Carol Burnett has my Joe. I suppose that's what she wanted . . . *and I hope she's happy*."

Without question, Carol was happy with Joe, and has been happy with him ever since. At this writing, Carol and Joe were looking back on twelve years of marriage. They have three youngsters of their own now—and their relationship with Joe's eight children from his first marriage has been far from the dire outlook cast by Gloria and Kip.

The children visit Carol and their father in their spacious Beverly Hills mansion with frequency and, while Carol may not be a mother to them, she certainly is the perfect hostess. On one of the very early visits Joe's brood paid to the Hamiltons on the Coast, Carol rolled up her sleeves, headed for the kitchen, and prepared a banquet-sized meal.

"I cooked sixty-seven pieces of chicken," Carol shuddered good-naturedly. "Afterwards the cleanup was *yiitch*!"

Things have worked out much better than anyone predicted a dozen years ago. Looking back on the attempts to scandalize her romance and marriage to Joe Hamilton, Carol says candidly:

"People still criticize me, I realize that, and I'm sorry

that they can't see my side, only what's in the papers. But you can't let public opinion run your life. Joe and I just hoped, very hard, that eventually everybody would be happy, and, thank God, everybody is.

"Besides my three girls, several of Joe's kids live with us—the others live with their mother in San Diego—and all of them are here in the summers. I call us Camp Hamilton. When I fix meals, I use the Army cookbook."

Neither Carol nor Joe could look into the future back in May 1963 and predict such happiness in the 1970s. Back then, their happiness was measured by day-to-day developments. And on that Monday, May 6, 1963, when they spent the first day of their honeymoon on the white sands of the beach at the Hawaiian Village Hotel, they were indeed happy newlyweds. They rode a catamaran, swam, and lolled on the beach.

But the honeymoon was all too short. For on that very day, back in New York, Carol's TV producer, Bob Banner, was announcing that the supporting cast for Miss Burnett's forthcoming ninety-minute special, *Calamity Jane*, had been selected and that rehearsals had to get underway soon because the musical comedy was to open a two-week pre-TV stage run in Dallas on June 24.

"We wanted to spend a much longer time on our honeymoon, but we just couldn't," Carol said. "Joe and I were sorry it came to an end so quickly."

The marriage of Carol Burnett and Joe Hamilton had caught many persons by surprise, but most of all *New York Post* syndicated columnist Earl Wilson, who had fallen victim to the comedienne's seeming habit of telling the press one thing and then doing another. For, only five weeks before the Juarez matrimonials, Carol had "confided" in Wilson:

"Joe and I are breaking up. We are concerned about the publicity. We think it is hurting his children and my sister Chris."

But we all know what happened on Saturday, May 4, 1963.

Was that another example of Carol Burnett's ambivalence?

Or was it just her woman's prerogative to change her mind?

8

No one could say that Joseph H. Hamilton wasted any time proving his procreative talents in his marriage to Carol Burnett. They were barely back from their honeymoon than a most astounding thing happened.

"I found I was pregnant," Carol says with a smile.

That revelation—coming as it did in mid-June, barely six weeks after the wedding—threw a portion of Broadway into panic, not to mention what it did to all the plans CBS-TV had for giving its million-dollar star prime-time exposure in the coming fall season.

"It was just an act of God," Carol rationalized.

But God did not indemnify CBS for the losses it sustained in cancelled commercials for Carol's planned fall-winter shows, nor did He make good on the fifty-thousand-dollar loss to the producers of *A Girl To Remember*, in which Carol was to have played the stage role of a young woman who goes to Hollywood to make one of those big lavish musicals of the 1930s.

It's true that Carol had tentatively agreed earlier to do *The Unfair Sex*, but she had had second thoughts about portraying a gal who runs a school that teaches damsels about the unfair sex—men. Producer Lester Osterman and composer Jule Styne, who was to have written the music for *Unfair Sex*, then offered Carol the starring role in *A Girl To Remember*, which was an original story by Betty Comden and Adolph Green.

Osterman and Styne flew to Hollywood in April, while Carol was making *Who's Been Sleeping In My Bed*? They talked her into a contract after Styne proposed to tailor the score to the big range of Carol's voice.

"It was a wonderful musical and I wanted to do it desperately because George Abbott had been signed to direct it," Carol said.

Abbott, Osterman, Comden, Green, and Styne also wanted to do it desperately. And between the time Carol finished her first movie and went off with Hamilton on their nuptials and the time she and Joe returned to New York, just about all the preliminaries had been ironed out.

Out-of-town playhouses were booked for road tryouts, Broadway's Mark Hellinger Theater was rented as of June 1, the opening was scheduled for November 23, and Osterman's On-Stage Productions Inc. had sold one million dollars worth of theater-party orders. Oh, yes—a full cast had been hired, too.

Carol wanted to be cooperative. She didn't want to scuttle the production. All she asked for was a little time.

"I was expecting the baby in February, so I told them I'd be ready to do the play in May," Carol explained. "In fact, I promised to show up at rehearsals in March."

But that seven-month delay was devastating. It compelled the producer to return the million dollars to the theater-party agents, and it made On-Stage liable for payments of twenty thousand dollars to the Hellinger for two weeks' rent, and a similar amount for guarantees made to the theaters in Boston and New Haven which had booked the musical for road tryouts.

In addition, eighteen singers and two actors who'd been signed for the company had to be paid two-week salaries amounting to four thousand dollars, and another six thousand dollars went for other production expenses.

The postponement touched off a major scramble by producers of other Broadway musicals and plays for the benefit evenings booked for *A Girl To Remember*.

If the people who'd counted on her to do the musical were disappointed, they could have taken solace in the fact that Carol Burnett had given them ample warning earlier about the vagaries of show business in a *New York Herald-Tribune* interview:

"You can't call your shots so far in advance. Who knows what's going to happen after this season. . . . It's a crazy wonderful bit, show business, and you never know what's going to happen. I guess that's why I love it so."

Carol's pregnancy didn't scuttle some of her other commitments, such as the two-week stage run of *Calamity Jane* that was to be showcased by CBS-TV in the fall as Carol's first ninety-minute special under the terms of her new ten-year contract.

Carol appeared at the Dallas State Fair on schedule for rehearsals, and the Western musical opened June 24. But it wasn't until November 12 that it was aired on TV. The next day the reviewers tore it to bits—and also praised it lavishly. Here are a couple of examples taken from New York newspapers:

Bob Williams, *The Post*—The exceptionally talented Carol Burnett mugged and clowned around with characteristic abandon last night in an undeserving and tedious TV version of the corny motion picture musical *Calamity Jane*. The story dragged, for most of the ninety minutes, from one lackluster tune to another.

Kay Gardella, *The News*—Only once in a laughtime does a show fit a star as perfectly as *Calamity Jane* fit Carol Burnett. The preposterous, noisy ninety-minute CBS-TV Western musical special about an untamed tomboy, who feels undressed without her guns, was a double barrel of laughs from start to finish.

But what did it matter how rough or how kind the critics were? They were very small voices in the sea of adulation and admiration that she was sailing on now. What was most important was that her fans loved her—that's what counts in show business. And for each and every time Carol appeared on TV for the remainder of

1963, Nielsen could tell the world the way it really was.

Actually, Carol Burnett's tremendous, indeed unprecedented, popularity has lasted and lasted and lasted, right up to this very day.

Looking back on 1963, Carol said:

"It was a pretty good year for me. Of course, marrying Joe was the best thing that ever happened to me. But professionally I had a wonderful year with all the plaques, silver bowls, statuettes, and parchments that were thrust upon me."

The most distinguished honor was the Peabody Award, which went to Carol for being "one of television's funniest and most highly acclaimed comediennes." Although the award given out by the University of Georgia and the Peabody Board was for her achievements in 1962 while playing as a regular on the *Garry Moore Show*, Carol received the prize in 1963—along with another from *TV Guide* and several more, including one from the 1963 World Television Festival held in Montreux, Switzerland. That was the Golden Rose trophy and although it went officially to CBS, it had been won by Carol Burnett and Julie Andrews for their *Julie and Carol at Carnegie Hall*. It was the first time in the history of the festival that an American production had commanded honors from the international seven-man jury that makes its selections of the best TV shows in the world.

All those honors filled a need for Carol, for she is highly sensitive to criticism. Carol readily admits it:

"It's a very personal thing being a performer. If I were a painter and someone said, 'God, I hate that picture,' I might be hurt. Or if I were a writer and someone said, 'I hate that book,' I might not take it personally. But when you're a performer and they don't like you, that's a very personal thing. It's you they're talking about."

When Carol's pregnancy became a show-stopper the *Garry Moore Show*, which Joe Hamilton was still producing, had to find a replacement for her. The search had started back when Carol had informed Garry she was quitting as a regular. But the urgency to locate a comedienne-singer to fill the gap wasn't as pressing then because Carol had agreed to make periodic appearances on Garry's show—at least four in the 1963–'64 season.

Now, however, with Carol waiting for the birth of her first child, a replacement had to be found at once.

Then lightning struck again. The bolt that had blasted Carol Burnett to stardom on Moore's show flashed again, bringing forth a performer with a remarkable likeness to the star she was replacing. In looks, personality, and performing ability Dorothy Louden seemed as close to Carol Burnett as an identical twin. And she wasn't on the show too many weeks before she began to resemble her predecessor in still another way.

"They certainly play romantic musical chairs at the *Garry Moore Show*. Dorothy Louden, who took over Carol Burnett's chores on the program, is dating David Geisel, who codirects it. David's wife, from whom he is separated, is the sister of Joe Hamilton, whom Carol recently married."

That was the lead item one fall day of 1963 in Dorothy Kilgallen's column and it touched off pandemonium at CBS. (We introduced David Geisel earlier, when we were speaking with his wife, Kip Hamilton Geisel, who's Joe's sister.) At first nobody could believe that that could happen—not again. Not on the *Garry Moore Show*. No one expected Garry to chaperone his people after the Carol Burnett-Joe Hamilton contretemps, yet it was hard to understand it happening again on the *Garry Moore Show*, that nice, clean, upright, funny, family-type program that it was.

How could that CBS studio spawn yet another romance involving Garry's star comedienne and one of the show's producers?

I was assigned to find out how it could happen. And here's what my investigation turned up after snooping around Garry's set and what I wrote after my inquiry:

"To our amazement, not only did we learn that Dorothy Louden and David Geisel are an item, but—hold on to

120

your seats—we discovered there was even more romance afoot on the Garry Moore set.

"Kip Hamilton—that's Dave Geisel's estranged wife—is dating William Harp. Ordinarily, you might not find it unusual for a gal whose husband has departed from the hearth to go out with other men. But William Harp, you must concede, isn't just any ordinary man. He happens to be Garry Moore's set director!"

With all that romantic rascality, it seemed that there just had to be something to those reports about the friendly "family" atmosphere on Garry's show. What else could have made it so conducive to all those warm-hearted attachments?

No question about it—things sure were happening in Moore's studio. And, incongruously, there was Garry, probably the cleanest-living guy in town. Yet, ironically, he was caught in a swirl of scandal or near-scandal that sporadically simmered from his show, and he was very much in the middle because it was his cast and his crew.

Unfortunately, the same titillating output wasn't being filmed by the cameras. Thus the show began a slow but inevitable downhill slide in popularity. Then finally it went the way of all shows that lose their audiences.

But, as it turned out, Garry Moore's loss was Carol Burnett's gain. Joe Hamilton wouldn't be out of work for long. CBS was prepared finally to have Carol do what she had always shied away from—her own TV show.

It was to be a weekly variety series that would be aired during the 1964–'65 season. Meanwhile, Carol's first child arrived two months ahead of schedule—in December.

9

When Carol Burnett was brought to St. Claire's Hospital that Saturday, December 5, she was terrified by her labor pains; her gynecologist had told her to expect her baby in February, nine months after she had conceived, ostensibly on or about May 4, the day Carol and Joe had been declared man and wife.

Carol's concern about the abdominal distress was that it could be a warning that she was aborting. Not until she was wheeled into the recovery room and had come out of her anesthetic slumber did she know the happy outcome.

The baby was a girl—a preemie who weighed a mere four and a half pounds. Carol spoke glowingly of wanting children through all of her mature life. Finally her dream had come true, but by the narrowest of margins.

For a time in the delivery room at St. Claire's it had been touch-and-go for both Carol and the baby, christened Carrie Louise. In giving birth Carol had a very difficult time. Then her period of recovery was prolonged and arduous.

Meanwhile, the baby didn't respond as well as the pediatrics specialists expected in the artificial environment of the incubator. For more than three weeks—long after Carol had left the hospital—the best pediatricians on St. Claire's staff ministered around the clock to the infant until the crisis had passed and Carrie Louise had put two full pounds on her tiny frame.

Carol and Joe went to the hospital every day and ogled Carrie Louise through the viewing glass in the nursery.

"She was such a tiny creature," Carol said. "I'd look at the other babies in their bassinets and they seemed like monsters next to her."

Then came a day in January when Carol was told she could bring Carrie Louise home. The happiest moment in Carol Burnett's life was when she went to the hospital with Joe to take "my little doll" home. They brought a dainty, lacy layette and a soft pink wool blanket that Carol wrapped tenderly around the baby for the trip home.

Despite Carol's flare for showiness and showmanship, there was none of that when Carrie Louise was installed in her nursery. Baby's homecoming didn't occasion a royal celebration. While Carol didn't exactly draw a curtain around the crib, she didn't go out of her way to show off her baby. Friends and relatives visited, but newspaper and magazine reporters and photographers who'd pleaded for interviews with Carol and Joe and for pictures of the new addition were turned down politely but firmly.

For the next two months Carol spent her days and nights in her twenty-second-floor apartment in what for her was a most unusual period of professional inactivity. But even with an around-the-clock nurse to care for Carrie, Carol's days and nights weren't idle. Her motherly instincts prompted Carol to hover over her infant almost to the point of pampering her.

"How else does a mother react to her first baby?" Carol asked. "I wanted to hold her and kiss her. She was a living doll."

The baby's premature arrival and the attendant crisis was in the past by Christmas Day, a joyous Yule with presents all around to and from Carol and Joe and Chris. Later that evening Carol and Joe attended a movie premiere just down the block from their apartment house —at the Victoria 72nd Street Playhouse. Carol had been biting her nails for weeks waiting for the film to arrive, for it was to be her first opportunity to see herself on the wide-wide screen of a movie theater.

Carol hated what she saw:

"I should have gotten the award for 'Worst Performance Ever Given In Movies By An Actress.' Why? Well, why does anyone stink? I was confused, bored. I missed the audience. Nothing was spontaneous. I had to show up at six A.M. and hang around while they put putty under my eyes and wait while they lit up and dressed up the set. By the time they were ready to shoot, I was ready for a nap."

The critics tended to agree with Carol. She didn't command the kind of praise she'd become accustomed to by her TV performances.

Herald-Tribune critic Robert Salmaggi found the film a "pleasant comedy romp" that provided "breezy escapist fare." He liked Dean Martin, but what he had to say about Carol made her cringe:

"Carol Burnett, making her screen debut as the counseling girlfriend of Elizabeth Montgomery, is somewhat self-conscious and a bit too animated. . . ."

By the beginning of March Carol had to take leave from her full-time duties as a mother. It was time to again meet her obligations to the entertainment world. The Broadway stage was waiting for her, and television was screaming for her return.

CBS wanted her to do another special. And while casting about for a proper vehicle for their million-dollar star, the network sought something that was "made" for Carol, just as, for example, *Hello Dolly*! was "made" for Carol Channing. No one had to look far to find the piece of stagecraft to fill Miss Burnett's ninety-minute time slot.

With Joe Hamilton as producer of Carol's TV shows (in conjunction with Bob Banner) holding out for a more perfect production than her first video special, *Calamity Jane*, the field of suggested scripts was narrowed to only one possible choice—a play out of Carol's past. That had to be *Once Upon A Mattress* since up to then that had been her only professional go on the legitimate stage.

"It was wonderful doing it again," Carol recalled. "Although I knew the script by heart, it was like a brand new experience because revisions had been made. And it was thrilling to be back on the mattresses being annoyed by that little pea."

In staging the TV version of the Broadway musical, the network had the benefit of all the polishing from those many performances by the cast. For besides Carol, other members of the original company were to appear in the TV version of the play.

Joe Bova had his original role as Prince Dauntless, Jane White as Queen Agravain, and Jack Gilford as King Sextimus. Then, too, Joe Layton, who choreographed the stage show, served as choreographer of the TV production as well as codirector—with David Geisel!

By now the game of musical chairs on the *Garry Moore Show* had played out its option. Dave and Dorothy Louden had stopped being an item, and the same was true of Dave's wife, Kip (Hamilton's sister), who was no longer seeing Garry Moore's set director, Bill Harp. Everything was hunky dory again, and against such a quiescent backdrop *Once Upon A Mattress* bounced through its rehearsal and production phases without a hitch.

When the last footage was taped and a June date was decided for its TV showing, Carol was free to answer the call from George Abbott, Lester Osterman, and Jule Styne, who had been working hard on the script and score for *A Girl To Remember*. There'd been many changes but the most significant of all was in the title. It was decided finally to call the musical *Fade Out-Fade In*. Carol was delighted with the new title.

"I had not been too keen about calling it *A Girl To Remember*," Carol said, "because wouldn't that have left the way open for critics to write, '*A Girl To Remember* is a girl to forget'? But under any name, the way the play had been written still was the story of my life. It wasn't meant to be—not the way *Funny Girl* was about Fanny Brice, for example. But *Fade Out-Fade In* did turn out that way.

"And it was my story—a plain-Jane who stumbles into stardom. The girl I played had an amazingly similar background to mine. In the show, the girl's father was a movie projectionist. My father was a movie theater manager. She was a movie buff who, upon arriving in Hollywood, spotted an oldtimer and yelled, 'Aren't you George Hackaway, the silent gangster star?' Then the girl in the show worked as an usherette, then she got a chorus job. I had done the same thing—but I was fired from Warner's Hollywood Theater because I wouldn't let the people take their seats during the last five minutes of the movie. And the girl in the show said, 'I was going to movies before I was born.' Well, so did I. Didn't my mother have to leave in the middle of *Rasputin and the Empress* because I was about to be born?"

Rehearsals for *Fade Out-Fade In* began March 23, a Monday, at 237 West 51st Street—the Mark Hellinger Theater, which had been rented briefly for the show before Carol's pregnancy caused the interruption. When she taxied from the Tower East Apartments on Seventy-second Street and walked through the stage door to the Hellinger that morning, Carol found an element of old home week.

There was George Abbott, as old as seventy-six but as young as tomorrow, eager to team up with the rubbery-faced clown he had helped to Broadway stardom five years earlier. But Abbott wasn't the only old friend in the wings. There was an even older friend backstage, the man who was to play Rudolph Governor, Carol's romantic interest in the show. He was Dick Patterson. Carol wrapped her arms around Dick and kissed him.

"We had worked together when we were students at UCLA," Carol said. "That backstage meeting was our first reunion in ten years."

Rehearsals went extremely well and after only two weeks it appeared that the schedules set at the outset could be kept—the road opening in New Haven on April 18, the tryout in Boston on April 28, and the Broadway premiere at the Mark Hellinger on May 26.

Then suddenly it was April 17 and Carol and Joe were in New Haven for the show's pre-Broadway tryout gig. But the car that took them up there had two other passengers—the sprightly, bouncy Carrie Louise Hamilton, all of seventeen weeks old at this juncture of 1964, and her nurse.

"I couldn't think of leaving Carrie Louise behind," Carol professed. "By having her with me, I didn't have to worry about how things were back home. She wasn't born in the proverbial theatrical trunk but she lived out of one at an early age."

Carol saw to it that on that trip her little infant had the most comfortable trunk money could buy—a tall English pram used at home to perambulate Carrie Louise through Central Park. There in the hotel suite during the company's one-week stand in New Haven and the four-week stay in Boston, the pram was the little girl's bunk.

The next night after their arrival in New Haven was Saturday, April 18. Carrie Louise was left in the nurse's care at the hotel as Joe escorted Carol to the theater for the curtain-raiser.

When the lights dimmed and the curtain rose, it didn't take but seconds for everyone to realize that *Fade Out-Fade In* was a topflight Broadway venture. Carol's opening number, "It's Good To Be Back Home," set the mood for the evening. For Carol, who'd been presold to the audience because of her television exposure as a zany clown, brought to the stage not only her gift for comedy but also a voice that on that opening night seemed to have taken on new strength and authority.

It was clear after the curtain descended—and after nearly a dozen curtain calls—that Carol, playing a plain chorus girl who is hired by mistake for the leading role of a big new film, had reached a new plateau in her career. The production was lavish and colorful. The songs were great. So were the performances of Jack Cassidy,

Tina Louise, Dick Patterson, as well as those of the other twenty-eight entertainers in the cast.

But Carol Burnett, playing with sympathy and hearty humor the eager showgirl named Hope Springfield, transformed into a star resplendently called Lila Tremaine, won the praises for her amiable zest and genial comic impudence on stage. And for that remaining week in New Haven and the four weeks in Boston, it was the same cheery output night after night.

"I had kept telling them all along that the delay would result in us having a much better show," Carol argued. "The authors had done a lot of revising work on it since the previous summer. And the revisions were all to the good. I doubt that they would or could have been made under the original production schedule."

An undisputed axiom of show business is that the applause-meter registerings in New Haven and Boston don't always rise as high as in that supposedly sophisticated locale known as Broadway. Thus even as the company returned to the Mark Hellinger riding the crest of rave out-of-town reviews, no one—except Carol—exuded total confidence that the opening in late May might not adversely affect the show's chances.

But Carol felt that a big, splashy, colorful musical was perfect summertime entertainment for New Yorkers. Moreover, there were all those visitors, too—for *Fade Out-Fade In*'s opening coincided with the commencement of the 1964–'65 World's Fair. And Carol was right. The New York critics were unanimous in their acclaim of the musical comedy—and also of Carol Burnett as its shining star. *Journal-American* drama critic John McClain enthused:

"The glamorous and ludicrous Hollywood of the thirties was given another going-over last night at the Mark Hellinger Theater, this one an opulent musical called *Fade Out-Fade In*, starring Carol Burnett and directed by George Abbott. It seems an assured smash."

Howard Taubman, of *The Times*, went so far as to say the musical "spreads enough good cheer to suggest that it will be around for quite a while." Then, speaking of the show's star, he said:

"When Carol Burnett is on the stage, the new musical is easy to take . . . Miss Burnett, in short, can dance and sing as well as clown."

The Hellinger's maintenance staff hadn't even vacuumed up the candy wrappers dropped by the first-night audience and ABC-Paramount was out with a recording of two *Fade Out-Fade In* songs. One was "You Mustn't Be Discouraged," the spoof of Shirley Temple and Bill "Bojangles" Robinson that Carol and Tiger Haynes did in the show. The flipside was "Go Home Train," a blues number which Carol had also sung in the show.

That was not the first time Miss Burnett's singing voice was cut into a platter. In 1961 she recorded a disc for Decca called "How They Stopped The Show," revealing a voice with a range, vitality, and style that bore comparisons to Judy Garland's flamboyant, lusty-voiced projections. That collection included such show-stopping tunes of the past as Ruth Etting's "Ten Cents A Dance," Ethel Waters' "Happiness Is a Thing Called Joe," Bert Williams' "Nobody," Vivian Blaine's "Adelaide's Lament," and Judy Garland's "The Trolley Song." Carol made no attempt at imitation, although she worked in the general vein of the original interpretations.

Carol had still another triumphant recording experience —Columbia cut a disc jockey promotional single from the *Julie and Carol at Carnegie Hall* special, "You're So London" and "Meantime."

But these achievements were merely extracurricular milestones that Carol passed along the way. Her real scoring was still being done on TV and the stage.

The night of *Fade Out-Fade In*'s thirteenth performance at the Mark Hellinger, Carol made Broadway-TV history. That was when CBS aired *Once Upon A Mattress*—the first time an actress playing on stage had been simultaneously projected on home screens in another Broadway production.

Critics applauded the video version of Carol's earlier

129

musical, which meant that she was now killing 'em on two fronts.

Less than a fortnight after *Fade Out-Fade In* had been declared a hit, Carol Burnett submitted to an interview by *The Times*' Joanne Stang. We quote from that feature just one significant statement Carol made which would come back to haunt her, as well as the producers and cast of the musical:

"I'm fatalistic. A long, long time ago I came to realize that the world does not revolve around me, or my career, or—in this case—the musical. It looks as though the show will run for a long, long time, but if it doesn't, it's been an exciting experience. . . ."

Five weeks later, on the night of July 10, Carol was in a cab going home after the show at the Mark Hellinger. As the driver was cutting in and out of the heavy midtown traffic, a car suddenly veered in front of the taxi. The cabbie jammed on his brakes and avoided a collision, but the sudden stop threw his passenger forward, producing an effect known as whiplash. It wasn't until after Carol got home and went to bed that she began to feel pain in her neck.

By morning the pain had worsened. When it came time to leave home for the Saturday matinee, Carol couldn't move her neck. She phoned the theater and said she couldn't make it. The afternoon and evening performances were staged despite Carol's absence. Her understudy, Carol Kemp, filled in. But it wasn't the same as having Carol Burnett on stage so far as the audience was concerned. The box office paid out nine thousand dollars in refunds.

"I went to my doctor and he put my neck in a brace," Carol said. "He advised me to quit the show because it was such a strain on my back and neck, since I had to dance and bounce around so much. But I didn't want to leave. I didn't want to hang up the cast and the producers. I had said that the musical didn't revolve around me, but the audiences were asking for their money back when I wasn't there. I knew that I had to go back."

130

The diagnosis of Carol's injury by her personal physician, Dr. William Zahm, was that she had aggravated an old neck problem—a herniated disc on the neck—and the pain was caused by pressure on her spine. Carol had suffered the initial injury on the *Garry Moore Show* doing a pratfall, then reinjured her back and neck while playing in *Once Upon A Mattress* on stage when she had taken one of many falls from the mattresses piled twenty high.

Although she had mended since, the sudden jolt in the cab caused a reinflamation of the neck disc. That kept Carol away from *Fade Out-Fade In* for several days. She returned after the pain subsided and continued to command capacity audiences.

But Carol didn't exactly set any attendance records of her own after she came back. In the next two months she missed no fewer than fifteen performances, and each time she didn't bounce onto the stage it was a nightmare for Lester Osterman and the other investors who had sunk nearly a half million dollars into the show. Seatholders invariably refused to see the show when Miss Burnett's name wasn't on the marquee. Even a substitute like Betty Hutton wasn't pulling.

The first to offer a clue as to what else besides a pain in the neck might be causing Carol's frequent absences from the show was Hollywood reporter Mike Connolly:

"Carol Burnett offered the producers of her Broadway musical the fantastic sum of five hundred thousand dollars to release her from the show. Carol claims it's one of those 'or else' emergencies. Meaning she just can't continue shooting her new TV series, *The Entertainers*, on the side, in addition to having any kind of home life with her husband and their child. She must really mean it, a whole half million dollars worth!"

If she wasn't really hurting, why Carol would have wanted out from *Fade Out-Fade In* became an even bigger mystery on the evening of September 25, when the TV series Joe Hamilton had put together for his wife premiered on CBS. *The Entertainers*, a one-hour variety show, left much to be desired. Even the presence of Bob Newhart, Caterina Valente, Tessie O'Shea, and some talented young performers new to TV did not excite the critics—nor the viewers. Though Nielsen gave the show a respectable audience rating the first night, the true indicator of its appeal came in the weeks immediately following.

The Entertainers went downhill steadily. The only bright spot in the first show was a comedy sketch by Carol and Dom DeLuise in the roles of a nearsighted couple, too vain to wear glasses, going out on their first date. DeLuise almost stole the scene with his antics which is quite an accomplishment for a performer playing opposite a comedic star like Carol Burnett.

Not everyone was sad to see Miss Burnett flop, however.

"I was glad *The Entertainers* bombed. I thought it might bring Carol to her senses and make her realize that she had a winner in *Fade Out-Fade In* and that she'd stick to it. But Carol had made up her mind to get the hell out of our show. And she didn't care how she did it or how much she hurt us. . . ."

That's what Lester Osterman told me. Osterman had some very unpleasant memories of the sequence of events that led up to *Fade Out-Fade In*'s closing after a Saturday night performance before rows upon rows of empty seats on November 14. That was exactly thirty days after Carol Burnett had announced that she was quitting both the Broadway musical and her own TV variety show to enter a hospital for treatment of her neck injury. Recalling those times, Osterman shrugged.

"The whole episode was incredible," he recounted. "We had the biggest hit on Broadway and we couldn't make a go of it because the star of our show didn't want it to happen. We were grossing sixty-four thousand dollars a week at the box office when Carol was with us. Without her we dropped down to sixteen thousand. I thought her attitude was unconscionable and I made a fight of it. But what good did it do? One of the year's biggest musicals became a bust anyway."

There's much more to the story. . . .

10

The peppermint-candy-striped walls of the nursery were like the backdrop of a Broadway stage in miniature, an appropriate setting for Carol Burnett, who was sitting on the soft pink carpet rolling a large rubber ball toward eleven-month-old Carrie Louise. Carol gravitated the ball toward her daughter and waited with a grin until Carrie sent it scooting back with a remarkable sense of direction. Each time the baby returned the ball, Carol cheered loudly and applauded enthusiastically. Carrie seemed to sense her accomplishment and basked in the riotous reception her mother gave her each time.

"She's just like her mother," Carol said. "Carrie's a real ham. Give her a hand and she'll eat up the compliment. This kid's a born trouper."

Carol was speaking to me. I'd gone up to get her side of the story about her absences from *Fade Out-Fade In*. She'd just returned from a three-week confinement in the Hospital for Joint Diseases. By now—mid-November 1964—Carol's aching back and neck had become a cause célèbre in Shubert Alley as well as in the courts of New York City.

When I made arrangements to see Carol I had, of course, told her that I wanted to talk about her medical ailment. But I'd also ventured up to the Hamilton's twenty-second-floor apartment aiming to ask a few impertinent questions about Carol and Joe's domestic life.

The rumors by then were rampant. Carol and Joe were supposed to have hit a rocky trail in their eighteen-months' marriage. The whispers on the CBS sound stages were quite brutal. There were mentions of divorce.

When I saw that Joe was at home, I knew that I'd better save my questions about the purported marital rift for last. From just looking at the two of them together I had the feeling that I was barking up the wrong tree. But looks aren't everything. Nevertheless, the questions I wanted to ask about the rumors could easily stir resentment, even anger—and Carol and Joe could show me to the door before I had a chance to find out what was going on with Carol's medical infirmities. I wished I had brought a photographer with me, for the picture of Carol and the baby would have been precious.

"Show the nice man how you can go to the bathroom all by yourself. . . ."

Carol was speaking to Carrie, of course. But the toddler didn't betray any inclination to answer nature's call. Carol then turned to me.

"I'm sure she doesn't really understand what I said, but it's a fact," Miss Burnett assured me. "Carrie can really go to the bathroom all by herself. But she does that only when the spirit moves her. Right now she's more interested in that. . . ."

Carrie had crawled over to a corner of the nursery and lay astride a five-foot snake made of rabbit fur.

"That belonged to me," Carol said. "It was a present and I was supposed to wear it around my neck. It came with a music box in the head. But then Carrie got hold of it and broke it. So now it's hers. She simply loves it."

Carol grimaced suddenly. She placed her hands against the leather brace around her neck, which she called a horsecollar, and tugged at it. Then she forced herself to straighten out and ease the center of her back against the baby's white crib. She rested in that position for fully a minute, and that seemed to do the trick. Then very

135

slowly she lifted herself to her feet and walked to the couch in the nursery. Again, moving in slow motion, Carol sat down.

"The doctor told me that I may have to go under the knife," Carol said with a shiver. "He wasn't kidding, either. He wasn't just saying that to slow me down—or to help me get out of my contract with *Fade Out-Fade In*, as the producers seem to think I'm trying to do."

She was referring to the suit just filed in New York County Supreme Court, the latest in a series of legal actions aimed at forcing Carol either to go back into the play or to get out of TV.

One of the litigations was brought by Actors' Equity, charging breach of contract. The actors' union ordered a disciplinary hearing on the grounds that Carol's departure from the show, which forced its closing, injured the other members of the cast, all members of Equity.

Another suit was filed by the musical's producers, who wanted to restrain Carol from appearing on *The Entertainers*, and also to stop the network from showing any of the TV programs in which Carol was cast. Carol was furious when she discussed the legal polemics exploding around her.

"They're trying to destroy me as a performer and subvert my personal and professional integrity," she fumed. "They're harassing me in an attempt to get a money settlement, although the show has closed through no fault of my own."

Make no mistake about it. In my view then (and I still hold to it now), Carol Burnett was being blind to reality. She had seen the gush of gold which had poured into the box office on the afternoons and evenings she was on stage, and she knew darn well that ticket sales when she wasn't there were strictly from poverty row. Yet she still refused to blame herself for the disaster. What she wanted was sympathy, compassion, and understanding.

"I'm receiving treatment here now," Carol said. "I have a hospital bed with traction devices in it and I am determined to do everything the doctor tells me. Everyone thought I was a hypochondriac when I was in the show because of the number of times I'd doubled over in pain. For a while I thought it was me—that I was unhappy with the show."

A Freudian slip? Could it be the truth—that Carol was unhappy with the show?

At the time it was hard to reconcile, for only a few months earlier Carol had been so emphatic in her enthusiasm for her stage role. And I quote:

"I guess this sounds very dull and Pollyanna-ish, but working at something you enjoy this much, and getting paid for it, is thrilling to me. It's marvelous when people appreciate you for just existing! There was a point in television" (while Carol was with the *Garry Moore Show*) "when I didn't know exactly how much money I was making, and I didn't care. When you don't have that much money as a kid you either grow up stingy—or go to the other extreme, and money doesn't mean that much to you.

"I think all performers are overpaid anyway, if you consider what people like teachers and research scientists make. It's the love of what you're doing that's important. That's so obvious with really great stars like Jack Lemmon and Danny Kaye. Why, their love of performing just *shines* in their work."

Without question, any performance that Carol Burnett had given up to then—and since—always *shone*. Even when she was hurting and/or was disgruntled and disenchanted with *Fade Out-Fade In*, no one could ever say that she wasn't giving one hundred and one percent when she was performing before the footlights.

I asked Carol whether she would try to get the play reopened if and when she felt she could take the strenuous activity required of her part. Remember, Carol had always spoken glowingly of the Broadway stage and constantly stressed that she would much prefer playing on the boards to doing anything else. But now, in response to my question, all Carol could do was shake her head.

"When it got to the point that the cast had to hold me

up and when the area around my neck blew up like Mount Vesuvius," Carol replied, "I knew I had to see the doctor. And he convinced me that I was leading myself down the road to ruin by refusing to take care of myself. And that's what I'm trying to do now. I don't think I can go back."

Carol, who was wearing tan stretch pants, a bright yellow turtleneck sweater with an extra neck of bright orange to dress up the neck brace, and black patent leather thong sandals, rose from the couch in the nursery, side-stepped little Carrie, who was crawling over her pet "snake," and ushered me into the tastefully decorated (French provincial) living room.

Joe was sitting by the window reading some papers. He looked up and smiled as Carol sank slowly into an easy chair, kicked off her sandals, and propped her feet under her, yoga fashion.

"You know," she continued, "there's a long time ahead of me. I'm still pretty young. I don't want to ruin myself forever. Joe and I intended to have more children right away—but I'm in no condition to have them now. You can see that yourself."

Carol put her hands up to her "horsecollar" again and stroked the edges to make her point. Joe returned Carol's smile and then turned to me.

"I'm worried about her health more than anything in the world," he said softly. "I don't give a hoot about the shows she'll miss—whether they're on Broadway or TV. My only concern is to see Carol get well. And I'm going to do everything in my power to make certain she does get well."

Carol said that her doctor had told her long rest—months of rest—was necessary for recovery. But even at that he couldn't assure her that the herniated disc would respond.

"There's still a chance that I may have to undergo surgery," Carol went on. "But I fervently hope I won't. That's why I'm being a good girl and listening to my doctor."

As Carol spoke my attention was drawn by a movement at the other end of the living room. Little Carrie was crawling along—bound for the bathroom! Carol's eyes lit up and she shouted triumphantly.

"See! I told you, didn't I—you can see for yourself now. My baby—she is housebroken, all right."

Joe's eyes followed Carrie across the room and his face glowed with fatherly pride. Carol turned to Joe and when their eyes met they broke into quiet laughter. A good time to get that rumor of a marital rift knocked down right now, I told myself.

I made no note of the exact wording of my question, although I wrote down every word of the response. But in words and substance, my query went something like, "My editor wanted me to ask you about some rumors—that you and Joe might be busting up, although it hardly looks that way to me. But, you understand, I have to follow orders . . ." I never finished the sentence, if indeed there was more to add to it. Carol and Joe both burst into laughter. Then Carol did the talking.

"Joe and I are planning on expanding the family. How can we have more children if we're going to bust up? Whoever started the rumor is a real mixed-up kid. But, frankly, I hadn't even heard of it."

As I left Mr. and Mrs. Hamilton I was convinced of one thing—there was no discord in their marriage. Joe's attitude and his attention to Carol, and Carol's attitude and her attention to Joe, betrayed only the signs of a happily married couple. Their interest in each other, their display of mutual respect for each other, and their total absorption in their marriage and daughter Carrie had to be unquestioned then—and I firmly believe it has been that way ever since.

But I did come away from the interview convinced of another thing—that Carol Burnett's illness was fatal. That is—fatal for *Fade Out-Fade In.*

For there was something in the way Carol said things, something about her body movements when she spoke, which told me that Carol, pains in the neck and pains in the back aside, just didn't want to finish out the run of her contract—to January 1966, fully fourteen months away from that mid-November day. That was just too much time to spend on a Broadway stage. Especially when Carol and Joe were already in so much trouble with *The Entertainers*.

I had the distinct feeling that Carol wanted nothing else to interfere with her TV routine, nothing to disturb her urgent dedication to save the show in any way she could so that her own reputation and career would survive. And so that Joe Hamilton's reputation and career, too, would survive.

From Carol's apartment I went to see noted labor-relations expert Theodore Kheel, who was acting as counsel for Leonard Osterman and Jule Styne. Thus far the legal battle with Miss Burnett had been a standoff.

Osterman and Styne had previously tried to enjoin CBS-TV from showing *The Entertainers* so long as Carol didn't perform in their musical. But Supreme Court Justice Samuel H. Hofstadter refused to act, although it had been argued in his courtroom that Carol didn't begin to miss performances of *Fade Out-Fade In* with any degree of regularity until August—when, significantly, they said, she was starting takes for her video series.

Meanwhile, my visit to Kheel enabled me to examine a response Carol had sent to Osterman and Styne after they'd fired off a telegram to her demanding to know when she would return to the play. Carol had written the reply in long hand on yellow-lined paper:

November 17, 1964

Dear Lester and Julie:

In answer to your telegram of November 13, I have no idea when, if ever, I can return to the type of physical activity I was doing before I went into the hospital—simply because the doctors themselves do not know.

I am sorry I got sick. I am sorry the play had to

close because I was sick. I am sorry you don't think I am sick.

Enclosed are the doctor's statements.

I hope when you read them you realize how unfair you have been.

You both know I kept going on in *Fade Out-Fade In* even when Dr. Kippmann, the doctor Lester sent me to, told me I would require hospitalization to treat this injury. You both know I did the show on several occasions with my back and neck medically frozen—and at times taped. You both know Lester once even asked me to do the show in the neck brace, saying I could cut anything out of the show I wanted . . . just so long as I showed up. This would have been as unfair to the paying audience as it would have been to me.

I have been told that I may someday have to undergo surgery if I do not respond favorably to the treatment I am now receiving. That, gentlemen, is scary!

I narrated a film last week, for about eleven minutes while in my apartment on my couch and in a neck brace. How you can equate this with two and a half hours of strenuous performing on stage, eight times a week, is beyond me. Again, I am sorry I got sick—and I am sorry you are mad at me for it.

Carol

P.S. Please excuse the stationery—it's all I had in the house.

There was no question about it now. Carol wasn't coming back in the foreseeable future. The show was suffering greatly at the box office, and so the decision was made to close it. And as *Fade Out-Fade In* faded out, Carol Burnett was catapulted to center stage of the theater world as a lonely, embattled warrior with not one ally. Ranged against her were Osterman and Styne, the League of New York Theaters (who look out for producers' interests), and Actors' Equity, Carol's own union.

They all contended that Carol had raised a fundamental issue—whether the arbitration machinery in the Equity-League contract was to be used in settling disputes between the star and the producers. On top of all that, the Broadway musicians' union griped to Osterman and Styne on behalf of the twenty-six orchestra members idled by the show's closing. The musicians protested "Carol Burnett's unwarranted action" in leaving the show.

None of this lessened Carol's determination, for on the day before Thanksgiving she fired her heaviest volley:

"Right now I'm mad at all of them. I have asked Actors' Equity to see if Lester Osterman and Jule Styne can be deprived of their right to act as producers in the theater because in what I consider an out-and-out power play, they are out to destroy me as a performer. They are harassing me in an attempt to get a money settlement, although the show has closed through no fault of my own."

Carol didn't exempt authors Betty Comden and Adolph Green from her tirade because Green had expressed amazement in seeing Carol on *The Entertainers* getting hit in the face with a pie and having a door fall on her head during the TV show's airing the previous week.

"The thing with the door had been done with a camera angle and a sound effect," Carol protested. "And I'd like to say to Adolph that I've never been hit with a pie in my life."

Carol was speaking now at a press conference she'd called in her apartment. And in the company of newspaper, magazine, television, and radio reporters, Carol let out a few secrets which confirmed my original suspicion—that she didn't want to do *Fade Out-Fade In* and would have done anything to get out of it.

Now, during the press conference, Carol was starting to tell it like it was.

"During our Boston tryout," she said, "I had tried to get the Broadway opening postponed until we could make some alterations in the production. But they told me they had a million dollars' worth of theater parties booked and didn't want to miss out on the World's Fair trade during the summer."

So there was an outright admission that Carol had been unhappy with *Fade Out-Fade In* to begin with. But then came the blockbusting confession:

"Yes, it's true. I tried to buy my way out of it for as high as I could have afforded. . . ."

That not only corroborated Mike Connolly's exclusive from months back, but it confirmed the producers' own claims that Carol had tried to grease their palms with monetary balm for her release. But Carol was no longer prepared to pay "even one cent" to win her emancipation from the show, since it had folded.

"I'm fighting back," Carol said, gritting her teeth. "I don't like to fight. But I'm fighting so that they won't do this to anybody else. And you know what? Jule Styne is still my favorite composer, though I should bite my tongue for saying it."

Carol had more to tell the press:

"I'd call a truce if an agreement could be reached with some degree of reasonableness—but I don't think these people are capable of reasoning. They are unfair. I think they want money."

Styne felt that Carol was menacing the very life of the theater, the star system, and, most importantly, the future of *Fade Out-Fade In*, which was now closed but whose producers continued to hope that Carol would return and the musical could reopen—something unheard of in Broadway annals.

Joe Hamilton took issue with the producers for placing such stress on the indispensibility of one actress, even if she happened to be the star of the show.

"That's a pretty sad commentary when they tell you that a show can't survive without its star," Hamilton protested. "That doesn't say much about the show."

That was all Joe had to say. But much more flak was due to fly from other quarters. On December 4—eve of Carrie Louise's first birthday—Carol was handed an early Christmas present from State Supreme Court Justice Thomas Dickens. His Honor denied Carol's motion to stay arbitration proceedings between her and the producers of *Fade Out-Fade In*. Dickens ruled that there was sufficient reason for Carol to be under obligation to the arbitration provisions of the collective bargaining agreement between Actors' Equity and the League of New York Theaters, the Broadway producers' organization.

Carol had contended that they couldn't intercede because her contract had no provision for arbitration. Well, she lost that round.

Now long afterward, late January 1965, *The Entertainers* was aired on a Saturday night, with a big surprise —Carol Burnett had returned. And in that particular segment they had a baby in a starring role. The thirteen-month infant gave a howling performance, for when singer John Davidson finished his serenade he was greeted with an emotional outburst from the youngest star of the show—a genuine bawling by the baby.

And that was Carrie Louise Hamilton's TV debut!

But even Carol and Joe's daughter's appearance on the show didn't help its ratings. By now one of the show's mainstays had thrown in the towel.

"I asked out because there was too little for me to do on the show," declared Bob Newhart as he washed his hands of *The Entertainers* and walked away into a future that would ultimately bring him his own show on the CBS network, a show whose Nielsen ratings would at times exceed Carol's.

Newhart demonstrated much insight in his candid conclusion of what was ailing the show:

"There are so many people on it, you just do your little segment and very little else. I didn't really feel I was a part of the show. Moreover, I objected to the rock 'n' roll acts that were being featured. I personally felt they hurt me badly. These rockers were attracting screaming teenagers to the studio audience. Who needs it? I was doing one routine in particular, and they didn't even seem to understand the material. They apparently didn't even recognize famous names from the headlines."

Carol had no comment about Newhart's farewell address, but she did explain why Carrie Louise had been on the show:

"I didn't plan to bring her us as a show-business kid, but I wanted to let her know what her old lady does so she wouldn't be shocked."

At this point the *Fade Out-Fade In* fiasco was far from over. In early February the entertainment world was handed the startling news that an attempt was to be made to reopen the musical on the fifteenth of the month—a feat no production had achieved before in the history of Broadway. What made the announcement all the more sensational was that Carol Burnett was to return as the star of the show.

That decision had been reached a bit earlier when Carol had finally capitulated at the series of hearings held by Actors' Equity and agreed to resume her place on stage until the expiration of her contract, in January 1966.

"I will do my utmost to perform in the show," Carol promised.

And with that Osterman and Styne proceeded to sink another hundred thousand dollars into the remounting of the show. The reopening expenses involved rehearsals, restaging, relighting, and some costume changes—especially for Carol, who had lost some twenty-five pounds since she had left the cast. Her outfits, every last one of them, had to be altered drastically or replaced. Then, too, there were cast changes.

Jack Cassidy, unable to return because of television and film commitments on the West Coast, was replaced by Dick Shawn.

Lester Osterman expressed hope for the success of the revived *Fade Out-Fade In*:

"We are trying to avoid acrimony and hard feelings. We want everybody to kiss and make up. We're certain if that happens we can make a go of the show."

Carol said nothing. When she finally went before the footlights on reincarnation night, she may have felt a contraction in her stomach. For if she could have counted the house through the glare of the spotlights beamed on her she would have seen that nearly three fourths of the 1,567 seats in the Mark Hellinger were empty.

The gross for reopening night was a piddling $3,085—against a possible sold-out-house income of $11,821. And with weekly operational expenses running close to $50,000, that was not the way of a hit play.

A few blocks uptown at the CBS studios where *The Entertainers* saga was being produced, things were not running smoothly either. A recurrence of Carol's neck ailment had sent her to a doctor, but she managed to make the evening performance of *Fade Out-Fade In*. But, the next day she called in sick, which made her miss that week's taping. Hamilton made the excuses for his wife:

"She got sick while we were having dinner. I told her she couldn't do the stage show. She said, 'I have to. I've got a doctor standing by in case I collapse.' I said 'I'm your husband and to hell with everybody!' I got her home and to bed. She had a virus."

Well, it didn't matter much that Carol had missed her date before the cameras for *The Entertainers* because CBS had had its fill of it; the network let out word that it was cancelling the series after the season.

A few weeks later, on the night of April 17, after a total of only two hundred and seventy-one performances (and a loss of more than five hundred thousand dollars), *Fade Out-Fade In* played its last performance on Broadway.

Only eight weeks after the musical had been revived, its star performer had again caused it to close. Carol Burnett, who had missed sixty out of those two hundred and seventy-one performances, said she couldn't possibly go on.

"I wanted to continue with the show," Carol said plaintively. "I told them I was willing to stay in it until June, maybe even into July. But my doctor, Alexander Berk, told me I had to take it easy from that moment on.

146

And that meant no work. He didn't want me to suffer the complications I had undergone the first time. . . ."

On that mid-April day of 1965, Carol Burnett was seven and a half weeks pregnant! Or so she said she was. . . .

11

Carol's detractors were quick to pounce on her after *Fade Out-Fade In* closed. They were saying her pregnancy entailed some rather hair-trigger timing. Biggest question raised was:

Did Carol know she was going to have a baby when she returned to the show on the night of February 13?

The point was very significant, for the reopened musical had survived only eight weeks. That slight time gap between the eight weeks of the show's second run and Carol's claim that Dr. Berk had told her she was seven and a half weeks with child meant she couldn't have been pregnant when *Fade Out-Fade In* reopened—not by three and a half days!

If she had known she was pregnant *before* the show reopened she could have faced legal action for withholding that information from the producers. But Carol said she was only seven and a half weeks pregnant. How could anyone prove it was longer than that?

I went to see Carol Burnett a short time after she had left the musical.

"Joe and I want the baby very much, and, of course, we'd both be delighted if it were a boy," Carol said. "But we'll take it if it's a girl, too. We both love children and I'm grateful that I can have them—even in my condition. I don't mind it."

Carol was in high spirits despite the pain she was still suffering in her neck and back. She guffawed as she recited some medical terminology that described her condition:

"I have traumatic disc pathology with secondary radiculitis and posterior ligamentous sprain, interspinous. How about that? In plain English, I have a slipped disc and sprained ligaments in my spine, which are pinching my nerves and causing all the pain and discomfort. And, believe me, it's going to add to my woes over the next six or seven months that I'll be carrying the baby. But so far I haven't encountered any special problems and I'm keeping my fingers crossed that I won't."

Just nine days after my talk with Carol, exactly eleven days after *Fade Out-Fade In*'s closing, Carol Burnett was rushed to Doctors Hospital. Her gynecologist, Dr. Alexander Berk, had ordered her there after she complained of severe abdominal pain.

On that night, April 29, Carol's dream was shattered. She lost the baby. Four days later she left the hospital. Then began a period of convalescence and a period to think about her future—as well as Joe's.

As 1964 drew to a close Carol wanted to forget that year, preferring to look ahead.

"If I could make three wishes for next year," Carol said, "I'd wish that my neck would fuse together, that everyone connected with *Fade Out-Fade In* would be happy, and that I could find a house with an upstairs and a downstairs."

Ironically, 1964 had started out as though it might be a good year for Carol. She'd been signed for the Broadway musical, she had that million-dollar contract with CBS, and the future promised so very much.

But then came the taxi accident and everything seemed to go wrong after that. Carol's career was doggedly off-course. Since she'd left Garry, misfortune seemed to trail her every step. And it continued even after she lost the baby.

"The Breakable Carol Burnett Broke Again," read the

captain under a photo in the *Herald-Tribune* on July 14, 1965. The picture showed Carol sitting on a couch at home, hands gesturing surrender and face posed in a "what can you do?" expression. Next to her resting against the couch were a pair of crutches. Her right leg was encased in a plaster cast.

Carol Burnett's "traumatic disc pathology with secondary radiculitis and posterior ligamentous sprain, interspinous," which had forced her to leave the Broadway musical, had prompted Adolph Greene and Betty Comden to rewrite the play when it reopened so that the star wouldn't have to do so much bouncing, and had also severely restricted her activity on *The Entertainers*, but did not stop Carol from playing softball with a bunch of kids out at Lido Beach on Long Island on that Saturday afternoon of July 12.

And during the game, if you haven't guessed by now, Carol broke her ankle.

"That was a strange one," Carol explained. "I was pitching. I reached to pick up the ball and felt a sharp pain in my ankle. They took me to the hospital. They took X-rays. The leg was broken in four places!"

The month of July wasn't a total waste, however. CBS, trying to get its money's worth out of its star now that *The Entertainers* had been cancelled, signed Zero Mostel, the star of Broadway's *Fiddler On the Roof*, to make his first network television appearance— and it would be on a Carol Burnett sixty-minute comedy-variety special to be shown in early 1966—a year that Carol, once again, was hoping would be better than the two preceding years.

CBS planned to tape the show in late August, after Mostel finished another commitment—re-creating his earlier Broadway role in the movie version of *A Funny Thing Happened On the Way To the Forum*. But Zero came back from England, where the footage was shot, and found that CBS had decided on a delay for two reasons: Carol's ankle was still quite tender; CBS was trying to make Carol Burnett's special something out of the extraordinary.

150

Or, to put it more accurately, Carol Burnett was trying to do that. And her way of making her special something really superspecial was to have the grand dame of comedy, the zany, incomparable Lucille Ball, on the show!

"I wanted her from the beginning but the people at CBS told me it was out of the question," Carol recalled. "They rattled off a long list of women they said they could get, but Lucy's name wasn't one of them. The deadline was closing in on us. I had to land Lucy or settle for somebody else. So I nervously phoned her. She asked me, 'When do we rehearse and tape?' I told her we'd rehearse for two weeks and then tape on February 27. She said, 'Sure, okay, I'd be glad to.' It was just as simple as that."

That's only half the story of how the cast for *Carol and Company* was roped. Did you get the impression earlier that CBS was responsible for Zero Mostel's appearance on the show? Not so. Carol gets credit for that achievement, too.

"Joe and I were having a social lunch with Zero in New York one day," Carol said. "Out of the blue, I asked him if he would appear on a special with me. And he said okay."

After Lucy was signed, CBS proudly announced its plan to present *Carol and Company* as Carol's fifth special under the terms of their exclusive long-term contract. The previous specials, if you've lost track, were *Julie and Carol at Carnegie Hall, Carol and Company* (with Robert Preston), *Calamity Jane,* and *Once Upon A Mattress.* And, as before, *Carol and Company* (costarring Lucille Ball and Zero Mostel) was being produced by Joe Hamilton for Bob Banner Associates.

In the meantime Carol's broken leg didn't allow her to get around much during the remainder of 1965. However, she did appear in early September as a thirteenth-anniversary guest on *I've Got A Secret,* hosted by Steve Allen.

Remember Carol's wish to find a house with an upstairs and a downstairs?

Well, Carol and Joe were doing just that in sunny

California. They settled on a Beverly Hills mansion—the very one that Betty Grable and Harry James had called home for so many years of their marriage. It was just what Carol wanted:

"That was the height of grandeur to me, being able to say, 'Well, I'm going out to the back yard now.' Funny, people do it all the time all over the country and never think of it as luxurious. But when you've lived in apartments all your life . . ."

Of course, Carol hadn't really lived in apartments all of her life. For the first eight years in San Antonio she resided with her family in a house with an upstairs and a downstairs—and even front and back yards. But Carol's memory of that experience wasn't too fond:

"On the outside we were surrounded by other houses, and on the inside we were surrounded by boarders. After that, Murphy beds seemed kind of spacious."

Jackie Joseph, the wife of Ken Berry, the *Mayberry R.F.D.* star, an old friend of Carol's, gives us an intimate view of Carol's early days in the house:

"It took Carol a long time to get accustomed to the house. I understand why. Even when she'd had money and was on the *Garry Moore Show*, she always lived in apartments.

"She was uneasy after she and Joe moved into Betty and Harry's place. At first, when she had people over for dinner, she'd sit at the table and ring a little bell for the servants between courses. But she'd always have to make some little flustered remark.

"It took a long time before she was accustomed not only to living in a house, but to wealth—and even to happiness and a whole family life."

Moving to Beverly Hills in October 1965 turned out to be a migration of the shortest duration.

"We had no sooner arrived there than Joe was hired to produce Sammy Davis Jr.'s weekly show for NBC," Carol recalled. "So we flew right back to New York."

However, they had no intention of remaining in New York permanently. But Hamilton's work would keep the family East for a while longer. Carol explained why she and Joe had decided to move to the Coast:

"Most television was originating in Hollywood by then. We wanted to be where the work was. That was why we had picked Beverly Hills instead of hunting for a house in Connecticut, which was once my dream locale for settling down."

Joe Hamilton was still busy with the *Sammy Davis Show* in New York when February 14, 1966, dawned. Rehearsals for Carol's special with Lucille Ball and Zero Mostel had to get underway. Since the show was being produced in Hollywood, Carol had to leave Joe and Carrie behind.

Filming in the movie capital was a rare experience for Carol. Except for doing *Who's Been Sleeping In My Bed?* for the movies, she had appeared before TV cameras in the film capital only a few times—when the *Garry Moore Show* did a stand on the Coast. Otherwise all her other TV appearances had been on New York's video stages.

Of the experience of that West Coast taping, Carol says:

"It's true, I had serious misgivings about working with Lucy and Zero. I was shaken by cracks about how we'd be at each other's throats. But as things turned out the three of us had a ball during rehearsals and the taping. And I was thrilled with the facilities. We used the studio where Red Skelton had been doing his show. It was a great place to work because you can establish tremendous rapport with the studio audience. The seats are placed close to the stage and the two front cameras were placed behind the audience, zooming in for tight shots, while the two side cameras were never between you and the people.

"It was like three Dinah Shores meeting under the mistletoe. Remember, the idea of having Lucy and Zero as my guests didn't come from the network. They were my choices. And we got along peachy, peachy."

Carol didn't stay in Hollywood after the show was taped; she hurried back to New York and rejoined Joe

153

and Carrie—then took part in a one-day, six-city whirl-wind tour which launched the nationwide Easter Seal Child Safety Crusade.

Frank Sinatra held no grudge against Carol for having outdrawn him during her 1962 date at the Sands; he put his Lear jet at Carol's disposal and she was off to Pittsburgh, Columbus, Detroit, Chicago, and St. Louis.

This is the first mention of Carol Burnett's charitable work, but I must stress that her tour for Easter Seals was just one of the many beneficences she has performed in the years since 1959—when she repaid her San Diego benefactor that thousand-dollar loan. Then, true to her word to him, she has made it a point—and to this very day continues to do so—of giving an annual grant of one thousand dollars to deserving young actresses (who must agree to the stipulation that she consented to upon receiving her loan, which is to help others when the recipient makes it in show business).

In addition to all that, Carol served as a weekly volunteer worker at New York University's rehabilitation center for handicapped children up until the day she moved to the Coast. The kids there cheerily referred to her as "that nut on TV."

By no means is that the extent of Carol's involvement in good works. Perhaps the most poignant of all of her fine deeds has to do with a teenager named Mary Jane Altomondo, whose leg was amputated in January 1964 at a New York hospital to stop the spread of cancer. Her courage through that ordeal drew the attention of reporters; stories about Mary Jane appeared in the newspapers.

After she left the hospital she was photographed making her way carefully on crutches into St. Patrick's Cathedral. She told newsmen that she had always wanted to be in show business—and hoped that she still could. She let it be known that the performer she admired most was Carol Burnett.

Carol read those stories and saw the picture of Mary

Jane hobbling her way into the cathedral. Carol picked up the phone—it took some checking first to get the girl's home in Bedford, Ohio—and called Mary Jane:

"Hello, this is Carol Burnett. How are you?"

"I'm fine *now*, Miss Burnett."

"Listen, Mary Jane, I read that you want to be an actress. Well, I'm taping my TV special, *Once Upon A Mattress*, next week. How would you like to be in it? Do you think you can come to New York?"

"*Yes . . . oh, yes.*"

"Okay, I'll make the arrangements. See you at the theater."

When Mary Jane arrived at the studio rehearsals were just getting underway. Her role—her first ever—was in a crowd scene at the end of the show. But Carol worked things out gradually and Mary Jane ended up with a small speaking part. Mary Jane's mother, Betty, recalled that visit to New York and her daughter's appearance on Carol Burnett's show—and some of the other things that happened to the Altomondos then:

"Carol didn't ignore anybody. She was very busy rehearsing, but no matter how busy she was, she always had time to throw a kiss, or wink, or wave. When you come to something new like this, you don't know how it is really going to be. But everybody, the director, the stagehands, the cast, the guards at the desk, the elevator boy, just everybody made us feel as though we were part of a big, happy family.

"We all went to a party at Sardi's East afterwards, and Carol had us to her home for dinner one night. It was just wonderful. They made you feel as though . . . well, you're here, you're one of us, sit down at the table and pick up a fork."

Mary Jane's brief brush with show business was over after her TV debut with Carol Burnett in *Once Upon A Mattress*. She returned to Bedford and finished high school. But she didn't pursue an acting career. She met a young man, married, and is now living in California. And while she didn't follow in Carol Burnett's theatrical footsteps, she has at least emulated her in another way.

Like Miss Burnett, Mary Jane is also the mother of three children.

12

March, 1966, was a very propitious month for Carol Burnett. Her special with Lucille Ball and Zero Mostel was aired and it was a big hit. And Joe Hamilton was emancipated from his bondage to Sammy Davis because NBC was taking the show off the air. Which put Carol and Joe into rhapsodical vocalization of a number called California, Here We Come.

Of Carol's show with Lucille Ball and Zero Mostel, one reviewer wrote:

"An ebullient troika galloped full tilt across the screen last night . . ."

So declared Richard F. Shepard in his *New York Times* review of not "Carol and Company," as the show was supposed to have been billed, but of *Carol + 2*.

Shepard's review took cognizance of the hasty, last-minute decision to change the title to *Carol + 2*, without explaining why. Word along TV Row was that CBS felt their other comedic star, Lucy, had too much stature to be slighted as Robert Preston had been earlier when he'd appeared in Carol's first *Carol and Company* special. For a while during the discussions, it was reported, CBS had considered calling the show "Carol & Lucy & Zero" or "Carol + Lucy + Zero." But Miss Burnett's side was said to have argued strongly that this was Carol's show—thus the compromise, *Carol + 2*, which still left Miss Ball and Mostel in anonymity so far as the title was concerned.

Whether these reports of behind-the-scenes negotiations

are true or not, the show itself revealed no attempt by Carol to hog the spotlight.

Shepard found that Carol "was too gracious to go by the numbers." She had given equal time to her "coconspirators," the man from *The Times* found. Significantly, because real talent always shows, Shepard and most critics around the country recognized that the producer-writer of the show was Nat Hiken, who had made Phil Silvers' *Sergeant Bilko* such an uproarious TV comedy success.

Let's hear what else Shepard had to say about *Carol + 2*:

"Miss Burnett had a field day, and this is reason to cheer. She sang beautifully, especially in a slow, sad version of 'Wait Till The Sun Shines Nellie.' The sketch in which her itchy nose led to her complete collapse was magnificent, and she and Miss Ball were thoroughly funny in a routine about making an eight-month-old baby say 'good-bye.' "

Of course, Shepard should have known better than to credit an eight-month-old with speech. The voice was dubbed. And if you remember the surprised look on Carol's face when the baby burbled "good-bye" it was only because she had recognized the voice.

Back in New York, Joe Hamilton had tape-recorded little Carrie's salutation and sent it to director Marc Breaux, who took care of the technical details of dubbing. Shepard also found that Lucille Ball was "in fine comic shape in her own style which matched but did not compete with Miss Burnett's." But the critic felt differently about Zero:

"It was a disappointment to see Mr. Mostel, a rare visitor to network TV and a tremendously funny man, used so sparingly. He simply didn't have enough to do. His one major skit, with Miss Burnett, was not up to the talent it was written for."

Now listen to Bob Williams' review in *The New York Post*:

"*Carol + 2* (or Carol Burnett plus Zero Mostel and Lucille Ball) was a rollicking good hour of TV sketch

158

comedy last night with hardly a minus that mattered. Perhaps the special should have been titled 'Carol Plus 3' (adding producer Nat Hiken, who manufactured the madness). Much the best of it here was Miss Burnett's marvelous clowning in a psychiatric sketch with Dr. Mostel. But that is not to laugh off their slam-battle as a 'Shut up! Drop Dead!' couple hooked on matrimony. . . ."

Every critic has his own view. So did some thirty million viewers. And because of their reaction, CBS decided that soon they'd rerun it.

Suddenly Carol was disrupted from settling into Betty Grable and Harry James' house. Emerson College, in Boston, had decided to present the first Alfred Lunt-Lynn Fontanne Award For Distinguished Achievement In The Performing Arts. And Carol Burnett was the recipient of that award.

Then exactly thirty days later, on May 25, Carol Burnett and Joe Hamilton announced to the world that they were expecting again!

"I'm thinking of taking a vacation abroad, probably in England, but nothing is set at the moment," Carol said to Kay Gardella of *The New York Daily News* in mid-March 1966. Miss Gardella had suggested that perhaps Carol could do a couple of performances at the Palladium in London to pay for the trip.

"Lord, no," Carol protested. "I'm not happy appearing anywhere except on television. To me, doing nightclubs is like going to the dentist. And with my teeth, that ought to give you a rough idea. If I were to go on a European vacation and at the same time prepare and rehearse for an engagement offered me, it would hardly be a vacation, now would it?"

So in late May, Carol Burnett, hardly settled in Beverly Hills, hied to London—and starred with Peter O'Toole in *Swing Her Up*. Joe went along and they remained in Europe through most of the summer.

Carol and Joe hit Switzerland on that "vacation," then went on to Venice and walked into a battery of cameras.

They were shooting scenes for *I Spy*, the Robert Culp-Bill Cosby series—for rival NBC. Although Carol was under exclusive contract to CBS, she nonetheless consented to do a walk-on for *I Spy*—for free!

"We walked right into the *I Spy* troupe while they were shooting in Venice," Carol chuckled. "It just seemed like a fun thing to do."

CBS didn't think so. But it was too late for them to do anything about it. They didn't know of it until Carol's face appeared on the rival network's screens during a late 1966 showing. Carol then got a light reprimand from John Reynolds, the CBS network president. Reynolds told Carol, "I wish, my dear, you would observe the exclusivity of our contract with you."

Carol's response: "Okay, John, baby, so what else is new?"

"We have scheduled you for another special," Reynolds replied. "We plan to show it in October. We're trying to line up Rock Hudson to sing a medley of popular songs with you. We're also going to have your old friend Ken Berry dancing, and Frank Gorshin doing ballads. And we've got a machine doing something surprising.

"Rock is going to play the wealthiest Texan in the world," he explained. "He returns home and finds two servants in his sumptuous home—his butler, Frank Gorshin, and a new computer which not only designs costumes but creates the perfect woman. And you, Carol, my dear, are going to play the push-button paragon. Isn't that a darling idea?"

Carol thought so. But when the show, called *Carol & Company*, was telecast the night of October 9, it fell slightly short of being something special. While her instincts for broad slapstick—mugging, screaming, falling—were at their best, the routine was too burdensome both on Miss Burnett and TV fans. As in times past and in times to come, Carol had to carry the show. Rock Hudson's debut as a singer made one thing clear—his classification in the Screen Actors Guild would remain unchanged.

Frank Gorshin, who was then a regular on the *Batman* series, playing Riddler, did impressions, and Ken Berry danced and sang. And although their performances were equal to their fine talents, the over-all impact of the hour-long show lacked the power and sweep of Carol's earlier specials.

CBS-TV's program chief, Michael Dann, who had viewed the tapes long before *Carol & Company* was aired, was less than pleased with the outcome. Other network brass, too, were unhappy with what they saw. They felt that Carol Burnett deserved better. And with the salary she was getting, her talents should be put to use more often.

After Dann and CBS president Reynolds held a series of meetings, word filtered out that Carol, like it or not, would have to do more for her keep. And the solution they arrived at was a weekly series.

Meanwhile Carol, who had always said she never wanted any part of a series because she didn't want the responsibilities and headaches, suddenly softened her line.

"Well," she said, "if I ever did a series, I'd want to do it the same way Lucy does—using three cameras and shooting right straight through with a live audience present. I'm still chicken about it though. It's kind of scary."

Scary or not, the ultimatum went out to Carol Burnett. And, as Dana said, CBS offered only two choices:

"We told her she could do a weekly situation comedy series or a variety show. She wanted the variety show because she felt it would offer a greater range for her talent."

Three days after *Carol & Company* was aired, CBS made it official—Carol Burnett would do a weekly grind beginning in September 1967. It was one of the best decisions CBS ever made. The weekly *Carol Burnett Show,* which to this day lights America's TV screens with a murderous comedy routine, transcended even the most glowing expectations of the network's optimists back in 1966, when they made up their minds to make Carol work for her buck.

Eight years is a mighty long time to survive on the tube, and what makes Carol's show's longevity even more fascinating is that the comedy-variety format peaked its way into extinction some years ago. Only a scarce few remain, and what new shows of this type the networks do put on fall into discard as quickly as they appear.

When Carol accepted the inevitable back in the fall of 1966, she voiced some criticism of herself and, at the same time, bared an eagerness to emulate Lucille Ball.

"Lucy is really a much stronger person than I am," Carol admitted. "I'm very wishy-washy. I'll take direction and let people have their way. Lucy, on the other hand, knows exactly what she wants to do, and no nonsense. She's undoubtedly the most honest person I've ever known.

"When Lucy complains, you know she means it. If a writer has written an unfunny line, she'll say outright: 'That's the worst line I've ever heard.' But she holds no grudges. She's just totally involved—and a pro. She even zips my dresses up and combs my hair on the set. I hope Lucy's wiseness and determination rub off on me."

Miss Ball zipped up Miss Burnett's dress and combed her hair when the two comediennes were teamed again, in "Lucy Gets A Roommate." That was Carol's way of paying back Lucy for appearing on *Carol + 2*. But since Lucy had done a full hour with Carol, and since Lucy's show was only a half-hour weekly series, well—the girls did what's known as a two-episode romp, which was presented on successive Monday nights.

The plot: Carol answers Lucy's advertisement for a quiet, dignified woman to share her apartment and expenses; after Carol moves in, her idiosyncracies surface, which weren't exactly what Lucy had expected in a roommate. Both episodes went over nonsensically well with viewers and critics.

All this time Carol was also trying to get accustomed to the new house.

"We had bought the house with the furnishings," Carol said. "After a while the bed that Betty Grable and Harry

James slept in began to give me a complex. And it wasn't fair to Joe. So we got a king-sized one. But then there's something else about living in that house. We have a great ghost. Every once in a while you can hear someone blowing a trumpet through a piece of Kleenex."

Carol enjoyed the beauty of flowers and the benefits of sun of Doheney Drive much more fully than she could in New York, where the separation of the two was stark; the potted plants were in the apartment house lobby and the barren roof was where Carol did her sunbathing.

In Beverly Hills, the spacious back yard brought those elements together, so Carol never missed an opportunity to relax in that tranquil setting. Well, it wasn't tranquil that fall day not long after she had moved in. She was invaded—through the hedges!—by a movie production crew.

"I knew immediately what I was in for when I saw the film director," Carol chuckled. "I recognized him because he was wearing knickers and a visored cap and was carrying a canvas chair with his name on it."

Before she could recover her aplomb, Carol found herself signed for her second movie, to be shot on location —her back yard. The director was a teenaged neighbor and the movie was an epic promoting the local school's fall dance. Carol graciously consented to be the "guest star" and danced a few turns with the students, voiced a dramatic plea for support of their social event—then brought out iced lemonade for her visitors.

Carol was asked if she was paid for her performance.

"Yes," she quipped. "They told me I could dance with ten percent of the stag line."

Since then, Carol has been the kids' favorite neighbor in a neighborhood heavily populated by movie and television stars. Carol would like to spend more time with the youngsters, but it's a full-time job handling her own brood and her stepchildren.

When they moved in, Carol and Joe had only Carrie. But not many weeks after the Hamiltons had settled down in their new home, Joe's two oldest boys, Joe Jr., fifteen, and Jeff, thirteen, came to live with their father and stepmother. And immediately afterward, Carol was ready to add still another member to the family.

On January 18, 1967, Carol Burnett gave birth in Santa Monica's St. John's Hospital to another baby girl, who was christened Jody Ann. The event followed six of the busiest weeks of Carol's career—she had filmed two TV guest shots, starred for a week in a Greek drama, and taped an hour-long network special.

About her latest achievement Carol said:

"We had wanted a boy but we got a beautiful doll of a girl. Well, I told myself, I'm going to end up being like everybody else in my family. Not since 1911 has anyone in my family had a boy. The others all had two daughters and gave up. But I was no quitter. I told myself, 'Give it a chance, Carol.'"

Carol returned home from the hospital with Jody Ann and had lots of time to get acquainted with her new daughter. Rehearsals and taping for the first of the *Carol Burnett Show* weekly series weren't scheduled to begin in Television City until early August. In the meantime, Carol had only one professional commitment to keep—a guest shot on the *Smothers Brothers Comedy Hour,* her final TV appearance until her own show made its debut after Labor Day.

Her guest appearance, aired the night of March 12, marked Carol's final stand as an itinerant TV performer, a status she'd enjoyed since leaving the *Garry Moore Show.* Although she had kept her promise to Garry and returned as a guest on his program more that twenty times, none of her reunions with Moore carried the sentimental feeling of her last appearance with him, in November 1966. Though she was advised not to go on because she was in the very last stages of her pregnancy, Carol wouldn't back out.

"I had to go on for Garry that one last time," Carol said. "That's the very least I could have done."

Carol felt that way because Garry Moore's show was going off the air at the end of the season. This time for good. Carol had hoped that by going on she might help breathe some life into it for another comeback. But the show had been getting low marks on the Nielsen scale week in and week out. Although Carol's guest appearances caused the charts to reflect a sudden revival of viewer interest, the occasional upsurges were only temporary.

What was heartbreaking about Carol's last fling with Garry was the speculation making the rounds of Television City that Miss Burnett's new series was going into the spot that Moore had occupied for so many years. When a reporter asked Carol for her reaction to that report, she voiced dismay.

"I don't think they will put me in the position of replacing Garry, who gave me my start," she said. "I would be horrified. I would have to be very hard-pressed to accept, and I might refuse."

During the early months of 1967 Joe Hamilton, who was to produce his wife's series just as he had all her specials, conducted a widespread search for writing talent and supporting cast. He planned to have Carol's hour lean hard on comedy. He plotted a format that would include a weekly situation-comedy segment, too, which would involve Carol with a TV "husband" and even a "sister."

By mid-May he had yet to cast the permanent members of the show, but he had made some strides in lining up guest stars. It seemed, from his early roundup of Lucille Ball, Imogene Coca, Diahann Carroll, and Gwen Verdon, that CBS was going all-out to make the *Carol Burnett Show* one of its biggest showcase productions that fall.

Yet the initial returns from the network's station affiliates were discouraging. Few seemed to want the show. CBS officials began chewing their pencils. However, their hopes were kept alive by Hamilton's promise to come up with an attractive package of supporting players—attractive enough to warrant eventual acceptance by most of the affiliates.

By mid-June the search for talent was completed. Harvey Korman, the versatile comic who'd been a regular on the *Danny Kaye Show* in the preceding four years, was picked as Carol's leading man, along with Lyle Waggoner, a handsome young newcomer then under contract to 20th Century-Fox. Korman was to be Carol's TV husband and Waggoner was her foil, as well as the show's announcer. The sister role was to be played by look-alike Vicki Lawrence.

The search for the most significant behind-the-scenes talent—the writers—resulted, ironically, in the recruitment of Arnie Rosen to head the staff of ten. Rosen happened to have been Garry Moore's comedy writer.

As the talent hunt ended and rehearsal call approached, Carol flitted off to New York for interviews with the press—which never hurt when a show is about to make its debut. Carol held court in her suite at the St. Regis to express her own feelings about having her own show, as well as to give reporters some idea about the format.

"I'm Nellie Nerves," she admitted. "I'm never at ease when I have to introduce a guest. I gag when it's time to say, 'My next guest is . . .' It's so bad, in fact, that something will be done about it right on the program. First, I'll tell the TV audience the truth. I'll tell them how terrified I am and that to help me overcome it, a young actor has been temporarily hired to help me with the introductions. Just as I say this, a gorgeous, beautiful hunk of man will appear on stage and the audience will know immediately I'll never get over my awkwardness. Of course, I'll never quite be able to pull it off. Something will invariably go wrong, like a broken heel, a strap showing, or maybe I'll trip at the wrong time. In any case, I'll be a puddle of water whenever that broad-shouldered Lyle Waggoner is around."

Carol then explained why she'd chosen to have a weekly situation-comedy sequence in which she portrayed a married woman with a younger sister who lives with her in a small apartment:

"It's an idea borrowed from my personal life. As an older girl who took care of a young teenaged sister, I believe the theme will have a great deal of appeal. This

166

way, we'll be able to treat some of the problems of our younger generation in a light, amusing way, but still deal with them."

Those jitters Carol spoke about would increase as the premiere neared. Yet her own nervousness hardly compared with the shakes the CBS brass suffered at show-time.

For when the *Carol Burnett Show* made its debut, no fewer than forty of the network's affiliated stations had turned the show down!

13

"It was on that hill that I received my first kiss from a funny little freckle-faced kid who wore thick glasses. . . ."

Carol Burnett was talking about a vacant lot in Hollywood where she and her childhood chums played king-of-the-mountain on a hill in the middle of what had become, by 1967, downtown Hollywood. The hill was still there, but the vacant lot had disappeared and in its place stood a huge hotel complex.

Carol was pointing out the scenery to her sister, Chris, who had moved to Los Angeles to be near Carol. Chris had quit college after two years and—well, we'll catch up with her past in a little bit. . . .

Pointing to the scene she was showing Chris, Carol said:

"It may never replace the *Romeo and Juliet* balcony to the world, but to me that hotel is built on the ashes of my first romance."

Carol had taken Chris on a sentimental journey of the old neighborhood which both had known so well in their youth. But the places Carol was showing Chris had undergone considerable change in the time since Carol had been a child. Carol was born in 1933 (Chris was born almost twelve years later), and it was at least another half-dozen years before she was able to begin shaping lasting impressions of the neighborhood. Since then, Hollywood had undergone drastic changes, just as neighboring Los

Angeles and, for that matter, communities throughout the country in the post-War boom and population explosion.

"The candy store where I used to sneak glimpses of the movie magazines is no longer there," Carol said later when she discussed that tour. "They've torn down the building and made it into a parking lot. But we found one landmark that both Chris and I recognized—the apartment house where we lived. It was still there."

When Carol and Chris approached the building neighbors poured out of their apartments. Many remembered Carol and Chris. And those who didn't certainly had no trouble in recognizing Carol.

"They rolled out the red carpet for us," Carol remembered. "They took Chris and me on the grand tour of the building. And, would you believe it, the apartment that I lived in with Nanny still had the Murphy beds and even the rack for hanging clothes over the bathtub!"

Because it meant so much to Carol, Chris came along for the rehearsals and taping of the first show.

"Carol needed moral support," Chris said. "She was terrified. I felt for her because I knew how jittery she always got when she'd have to sing or introduce guests. But I was very proud of my big sister as I watched her up there on the stage. She was magnificent."

On Monday night, September 11, 1967, Carol and Joe were at home. Eight-month-old Jody Ann was tucked in her crib. Joe's two sons, Joe Jr. and Jeff, were horsing around with their little stepsister, Carrie Louise, who'd been given permission to stay up late that night "to see Mommy on television." At 10 P.M. sharp everyone gathered in the den. Potato chips and popcorn were on the coffee table for everyone, and there were Cokes for the boys and Carrie, dry martinis for Carol and Joe.

"Ooh, I think I'm gonna die, Joe," Carol squirmed.

"Oh, shut up, Carol!" Hamilton shot back.

The *Carol Burnett Show* was on!

After the music faded Carol saw herself opening the show with an intimate monologue, much in the style of Bob Hope. Then she introduced Lyle Waggoner. Only

169

Carol and Joe laughed at Carol's quip because only they were old enough to know who the butt of Miss Burnett's crack was:

"Do you know we almost hired Harry Von Zell?"

That was a precious early line in the show. Carol had faked a faint over the tall, handsome Waggoner. That brought uproarious laughter from the studio audience, which is so much better than the canned variety. The folks at home also got a kick out of the show in the early going. But would they continue to enjoy it?

Yes. For when Jim Nabors, Carol's guest star, came on with the star of the show in a skit about two accident-prone people on vacation at a ski lodge, the house came down. They made beautiful bruises together, with Carol ending up with her arm in a cast and Nabors having a plaster-of-paris casing on his leg.

The real test came when the situation-comedy segment was presented—Carol and her "husband" Harvey Korman, the married couple blessed with Carol's teenage "sister" living with them. It was like a page out of Carol's own life when she was married to Don Saroyan and Chris had come to live with them.

The episode called upon a real-life situation for laughs, and anyone familiar with a teenager's ways of bugging grownups had to appreciate the inaugural showing of Harvey and Carol and Vicki Lawrence. Vicki's repeated trips to the refrigerator and her tomboy manifestations were a continual frustration to her married chaperones, who were yearning for a little time alone. Finally, this conversation ensued:

"Why doesn't she go out and protest something?"

"Shhh. She's sensitive about never having been arrested."

When Vicki was fixed up with a date, Carol advised her to be "helpless, feminine, and slouch"—because the young man was so much shorter than she.

"You're supposed to be a girl, not King Kong," Carol admonished Vicki.

Miss Burnett drew more laughs with her other lines,

but there came a point where the humor produced by Arnie Rosen's writing team approached what some critics defined as "humor with political implications" and which supposedly "bordered on the vicious."

What that was all about concerned a satire—on Shirley Temple's plunge into politics and F. Lee Bailey's new TV series. But that was the view of some TV reviewers who worked for newspapers leaning toward the Republican-Conservative-party sides. Those grinding out copy for the Democratic-Liberal-party-oriented publications had had nothing but glowing comments about those sketches. In fact, George Gent of *The New York Times* suggested that the "devastating and hilarious take-off of Shirley Temple" might be used by the California Democrats against the former child star in her campaign for election to Congress—which, incidentally, she lost.

"I was so relieved after seeing the show," Carol said. "I liked it. Joe liked it. Joe Jr. and Jeff liked it. And even Carrie liked it, I think. But I was jittery. To do a show every week was, oooh . . . rough, to say the least."

But Carol managed to do that show through the rest of the 1967–'68 season, and through all the years since. Yet at the outset there was no clue that the show would succeed as it has, for the morning after the premiere Carol was to learn the awful truth about those forty CBS network affiliates that turned down the show.

Carol was shaken by the news:

"I know for a fact that CBS had kept from me the stations' indifference to my show because they didn't want to worry me. Believe me, I would have worried. I was terrified enough being a hostess on a whole hour of TV, but when I heard that I wasn't wanted, I *was* terrified."

Miss Burnett's fears proved groundless. Within a week nineteen of the forty stations that had spurned her show were begging to have it. By the middle of November all forty stations were telecasting the *Carol Burnett Show*. The Nielsen numbers had put Carol's show on every CBS network affiliate's Monday night program roster.

Even more remarkable, Carol had outdrawn her two

chief competitors on rival networks. That was the ABC-TV *Big Valley* series and her two chums Robert Culp and Bill Cosby in *I Spy* on NBC. Since Carol had done a walk-on for Culp and Cosby the previous year in Europe, she thought she could have them on her show. But when she was slotted as their direct competitor on Monday night primetime, she learned that CBS would never allow them on as guests—nor would NBC let them do it. That ended that.

For the remainder of the *Carol Burnett Show*'s run in the 1967–'68 season, it was just like gangbusters. Each Monday night Carol and company exploded their audiences into racketing barks of laughter. There was never a let-up. For the first time since Lucille Ball had thundered across the TV screen and established herself as the queen of comedy, a rival female laugh-getter had infiltrated the tube with a successful show of her own.

Fan mail for Carol and the other performers poured into CBS stations all over the country. Everyone raved about the sketches, about the rib-tickling humor, and, of course, about Carol. But the postcard and letter writers had one uniform complaint:

Why, they wanted to know, did the show go on so late at night?

The squawks were from parents who didn't like the idea of their kids going to bed at 11 P.M. Well, that was something to think about—and in time CBS would remedy that.

No one was more astounded at the success of the show than the girl with the toothy grin and the goofy-Cousin-Clara look.

"I was more surprised than the network," Carol admitted. "I thought, well, I'll get thirty weeks out of this and it'll be cancelled."

Although I said earlier that CBS more or less gave Carol an ultimatum to do the show, there seems to be a difference of opinion so far as Carol is concerned. Sure, the network had pressured her from the very outset of her ten-year contract to do a weekly show, but she resisted and went on to do only specials—only six by actual count, over the first five years of that pact—and the ill-fated *The Entertainers* series.

What, then, if not a demand by CBS to do the show (as I was told) made Carol change her mind?

Actually, Carol claims, it wasn't a matter of *changing* but, rather, *making up* her mind. And Carol credits Joe Hamilton for helping her in that decision.

"When the fifth year came," Carol said, "my husband said, 'Are you going to push the button or not?' Well, I thought it over. For about twenty seconds. No, I'm serious. I'm chicken—that's why I put it off for five years—and I knew if I started thinking, I'd say no.

"We considered situation comedy because I know that I'm best as a comic actress. Then I said, what the hell, let's try variety with lots of sketches. If by some wild chance it succeeds, it will be twice as much of a coup. Nobody wanted us at first. In New Orleans we were on at like midnight. Then the ratings started to build—and build! And it all seemed so easy. . . ."

And, of course, the ratings have continued to build and build—right up to the 1974–'75 season. Eight happy, successful years. But Carol Burnett readily admits that none of this could have happened if it weren't for Joe Hamilton, her "boss," as she calls him. In truth, he is her boss—at home and on the set. And Carol, who once expressed a desire to be an aggressive-leader-type like Lucille Ball in the production of her show, has not let the other redhead's style rub off on her.

Carol gives us an intimate glimpse into the way things go on the show:

"I don't order Joe and the staff around. I have nothing to do with running the show. The only place I stick my nose in is the matter of sound. I am a sound bug. To me, a sound is funny only when it is not funny. Like, when I'm punched in the stomach I don't want a *varoom,* a bass-drum sound. That's not my style. I want a real punch-in-the-gut sound, so that the audience winces, but laughs harder afterward. I've had the same sound engineer for years, and we work at it for hours, until it's real. Otherwise, Joe makes all the decisions. He makes the schedule, and if he says to get up early, I *git*!"

Joe, however, is never that harsh, for he knows his wife's kooky sleeping habits—because Carol is a night owl, if not indeed an insomniac.

"When I lived in the apartment in New York," Carol said, "I got up in the middle of the night and Glamorened the rug. Or sometimes I'd write letters into the wee hours. Or take hot baths. None of it worked. Now I get up and stand on my head" (Carol is doing yoga these days).

"Or I get in bed with my remote control and watch three old movies in a row. That's my idea of an orgy. One night I saw *Gaslight, Sweet Rosie O'Grady,* and—oh, my God, I can't even remember the third! I know them all by heart, but it doesn't matter. There I am, 4 A.M., standing for the national anthem. 'Goodnight, Betty Grable and John Payne. I love you.'"

Carol never has to fear that Joe will shake her awake an hour after the sermonette. The secret's in the scheduling of rehearsals and also in Carol's well-planned daily routine and work habits.

"I don't get up early," Carol assures us. "We only rehearse afternoons. Fridays, our long day, we dress-rehearse for one audience, tape for another. We're so well organized nobody ever has to stand around waiting, especially the guests. I've got a music system in my car, and I learn my songs while I drive to the studio.

"I'm telling you, I have a lot more time with the kids than most working mothers, and because I *am* working, I'm twice as turned-on for them. Here I go, Goody Two-Shoes, but honestly, I wake up looking forward to work. Everybody on the show is like that."

Eleven days after Jim Nabors had helped launch Carol's first show, the *Gomer Pyle—USMC* series had a very funny guest in a very funny plot about a woman

174

Marine Corps corporal, Carol Barnes, who misinterprets Gomer Pyle's excitement over his date with Lou Ann Poovie, played by Elizabeth MacRae.

After an angry Lou Ann has given Gomer the brush for breaking two dates, Carol, still not understanding, goes with Gomer to see Lou Ann and explain the situation—the corporal's way. Carol Barnes was played by Carol Burnett, and her appearance on Jim Nabor's show was more than mere courtesy of repaying a guest visit with a guest visit.

Jim happens to be Carol's and Joe's nearest and dearest friend. And vice versa, or, as Nabors puts it:

"Carol and Joe are like family."

Actually, Jim is a part of the Hamilton family, and has been since Carol and Joe settled in Beverly Hills. Carol had met Nabors years before—when she had come to the Coast to do some segments of the *Garry Moore Show*. That was before she and Joe began romancing.

Nabors was singing at The Horn, a nightclub in the Hollywood area where Andy Griffith "discovered" him, and Carol came in with Bill Dana one night. The sight of Miss Burnett in the audience jolted Jim.

"She was a big star then and it took quite a while before I got up the nerve to go over to her table and introduce myself," Nabors related. "I just said that I was a big fan and so on and so forth. She was very, very nice —like she always is with people. But she doesn't remember at all."

Carol says the first time that she ever remembers seeing Jim Nabors was when she was in the Hospital for Joint Diseases in New York with that neck and back trouble. She saw an episode of *Gomer Pyle—USMC* and "I almost fell out of bed laughing."

Carol penned Nabors a letter:

"I think you're superb. I'm sold on the show . . . I'm a fan and I'll be watching. Keep up the good work. . . ."

"When I got that letter," Nabors said, "I thought, 'Oh, g'wan! It's somebody puttin' me on.'"

Some months later, while Carol was rehearsing a scene for *The Entertainers* (in the ballroom of the Park Sheraton Hotel in New York), someone said that Jim Nabors was in the coffee shop. Carol dashed downstairs but didn't find him. Back at rehearsal, Carol was doing a scene in which she had to crawl on her hands and knees to the exit.

Carol describes what happened then:

"I got to someone's leg and I looked up—and it was Jim Nabors! He was standing in the wings with a couple of other people. I just screamed. I was like a teenager meeting The Beatles. I threw out my arms and said, 'Ooooooh! There you are! Oh, my Lord! I *love* you and I *love* the show!' I think I came on so strong I probably frightened him half to death!"

The next time Carol saw Nabors was after she and Joe and Carrie Louise went West. Carol and Joe invited Jim to dinner and they wound up at a piano bar—and almost got arrested. They'd been singing and at 2 A.M., ginbill closing time in California, the manager saw what a good time they were having and suggested that they hide in the restrooms until he got rid of the other patrons, then come back and sing all they wanted to.

"Great!" Carol says she shouted. "So I hid in the ladies' room and Joe and Jim went to the men's room. After the manager cleared everybody out, we got around the piano and we sang so loud that, about 3 A.M., there was a loud banging on the front door, and then a voice: 'Police! Open up!' We had been doing Jeanette MacDonald and Nelson Eddy duets, and Jim was singing grand opera. We must have been rattling the cups a mile away. Anyway, we got rid of the cops."

The first time Carol Burnett and Jim Nabors appeared together professionally was before a private audience of CBS executives at a network-station-affiliates convention. In that skit they knocked each other down, forgot their lines—and broke up altogether. Their audience broke up, too.

Their next professional appearance together was on the *Carol Burnett Show* premiere, followed by their skit on the *Gomer Pyle—USMC* series. Many others were to follow.

By New Year's Eve Carol could look back with satisfaction on the year past, and ahead to 1968 with hope and cheer.

Sixteen segments of the *Carol Burnett Show* had been televised and CBS executives were looking down from their paneled suites with astonishment because they never thought the series would go into its second half of the season—not after the way it had started out.

Now they were patting each other on the back for their foresight, decisiveness, courage, and aggressiveness in putting Carol Burnett into her own weekly variety show.

Eight years later, they're still congratulating each other.

As for Carol Burnett—well, it had been a short period of inactivity over the Christmas holidays. She had torn a leaf from Garry Moore's production style and filmed her holiday shows long in advance, giving everybody a chance to rest and enjoy the holidays.

Christmas was spent at home but New Year's Eve called for a really special celebration. Jim Nabors dreamed up the idea of spending the holiday at a lodge belonging to the owners of Harrah's Club in Lake Tahoe. Carol and Joe brought Carrie along but Jody Ann, barely a year old, stayed home with her nurse and Joe's baby-sitting sons. So what did Carol and Joe and Carrie and Jim do at the resort?

"We went sledding for a couple of hours and then we came back to the house and watched TV," Carol related. "I kid you not. There was one movie we just adored—*Now Voyager*, starring Bette Davis. Jimmy and I sat there crying our eyes out for that poor woman and all she had to go through. Joe got hysterical, laughing at us.

"On New Year's Eve we all felt the same way. We didn't want to go anywhere. But Jack Jones was appearing at Harrah's so we did catch the special New Year's show. The minute it was over we went backstage and told Jack how marvelous he'd been and wished him a happy New Year . . . and then it struck midnight and everybody in the club started tooting the horns and so forth.

"And we split! We were back at the lodge at ten after twelve—watching Guy Lombardo on TV!"

Jim Nabors' mental picture of Carol Burnett is an indelible imprint in his mind:

"This may sound ridiculous, but I *see* her watching TV. She is the world's biggest TV fan. She watches everyone and everybody. She especially loves old movies."

What is Jim Nabors' over-all view of Carol Burnett? What kind of person is she really—at work and at home? His evaluation:

"Pretty terrific. She has very little ego-type thing. I don't know how to explain it except that she has a wonderful way of putting everything in its proper place. Like at work, she's a fantastic professional. She does her thing better than anybody else. And yet at home, she isn't 'on.' Sure, she constantly has the humor going— she just naturally thinks that way—but she's never *performing*. She's simply a marvelous mother to her kids and a great wife to Joe.

"Yes, she can cook, too. I'd say her best dish is meat loaf. But it's with those kids that she shines. After a while, Joe's kids lived in a little guest house in back of the main house. There they could have all the privacy they needed. And, of course, there are Carol and Joe's little ones. Then, too, their young friends visit often—and not infrequently Joe's other children will be visiting.

"So there has always been activity, to put it mildly. But it's perfect for Carol. She loves *all* those children, she really does. You'd just have to be around for ten minutes to know that. It's hard to think of what to say about Carol. If you're lucky enough to spend any time with her, you'll discover that she's a very normal person.

"She enjoys very ordinary things. For example, if you come over to her house during a day when she's not working, you'll most likely find her outside playing baseball with the kids. I will say that everything she does, she really goes at it. You know, she broke her ankle playing ball with the kids a few years ago."

What does Jim Nabors think of Carol and Joe's marriage?

"Carol and Joe have one of the happiest marriages I've ever seen. When you've said that, what else is there to say?

"Actually, I became friends of Carol and Joe's at the same time. Joe and I have quite similar tastes in a lot of things. I'm very fond of him. He's got the same sense of humor as Carol and I. For example, we can see something ordinary on the street and we'll both think the same thing and break up laughing. Maybe Joe is a little more serious . . . no, he isn't really. He's as wacky as we are, except he can stay straight where Carol and I fall over giggling. Joe can maintain his composure better, but he's just as crazy.

"Carol has a lot of very Southern mannerisms. She reminds me quite a bit of the girls back home" (Nabors is from Sylacauga, Alabama). "It's hard to describe. You just feel very comfortable with her. Anybody who doesn't hit it off with Carol needs to have his head examined. I'm serious. I feel like I grew up with her—that's the way it is with us. She's from Texas, so we both have had a real folksy-type background.

"And another thing—I've always considered Carol to be very, very pretty. *Natural* pretty. She's one of the prettiest girls around, I think. She's always making faces, which is part of her talent as a comedienne, but if you just sit in a room and look at her, she's extremely attractive. To elaborate any further would be kind of incestuous . . . I mean, we're like *family*—like brother and sister, you could say."

A while back, Jim Nabors spoke about Carol's great love for children. He also reported on the New Year's holiday at Lake Tahoe. But it may have been an incomplete account of happenings on that outing. Maybe Jim and Carol and Joe did spend a lot of time in front of the TV. But then consider this:

Not long after Carol and Joe were back in Beverly Hills from that trip they let it be known that they were looking forward to another blessed event. . . .

14

As Carol Burnett rode the crest of her first season's success, she suddenly was named UCLA Alumna of the Year. Carol was one of the first women to receive this honor. She attended a splashy bash on May 25 to take home that honor—after breaking up the gathering with her side-splitting gags and cracks which, incidentally, are slightly different than the ones you hear on her telecasts. To illustrate the point, let's move ahead to May 1973.

Carol was in New York to collect still another award, this one from the Friars Club as Entertainer of the Year. In this instance she was only the third woman ever to be so honored by the theatrical fraternity. (Dinah Shore, the only other member of her sex to have headed her own successful TV variety hour, and Barbara Streisand, who is known for other entertainment-world achievements, were the previous recipients of the Friars' annual award.) At any Friars' shindig that's held to honor a celebrity, the modus operandi is to roast, roast, and roast that celebrity. Well, to give you an idea of how it went for Carol:

Harvey Korman: I once asked Carol, "How do you feel about breast feeding?" She said, "I'll feed 'em anything as long as they'll grow."

Walter Matthau: Carol's not really a great star. Talented but not a great star. Of course, she was so nice and so sweet—after Barbara Streisand. And, moreover, I think Carol Burnett is beautiful. . . ."

Matthau was suddenly interrupted by a shout.

"Bullshit!"

That was Carol. And it broke up the audience. Later, she had the Friars falling out of their chairs, especially when she let Harvey Korman smash a cream pie in her face. Still later, columnist Earl Wilson went backstage to offer Carol congratulations.

"Come back in a half hour," someone from Carol's dressing room shouted. "It'll take her that long to get the stuff out of her hair and ears."

While in town, Carol let her down-to-earth self show some more. A reporter asked her whether her recent TV naughty-lady movie takeoffs weren't risqué, especially for someone who had built up an Ivory soap image in her video performances.

"Not compared with those dirty soap operas," Carol cracked. "We're G-rated compared to daytime TV."

She was then asked whether she had a second career in mind.

"I should say a stunt woman in stag movies," Carol offered. "But I'd really like to be a schoolteacher for kids aged six to eight. They haven't heard all my jokes."

We're back to the month of August 1968, and Carol Burnett is talking to *New York News* TV critic Kay Gardella, who is visiting Carol at her Beverly Hills home.

"Well, here I am," Carol said to Kay. "I don't care what it is, just so it's a baby. I never had a boy, though. All I know about them is you have to duck when you change their diapers."

Miss Gardella was the last reporter to speak with Carol before she headed to St. John's Hospital to have her baby. Carol entered the hospital a few days later, on the fourteenth of the month, and just hours afterward she gave birth to Erin Kate—another girl.

Carol was right. She couldn't buck her family's sixty-seven-year tradition of begetting only girls.

When Carol returned home with Erin Kate she was

not under any great pressure to prepare for rehearsals and taping of her first fall TV show. She'd already taken care of that detail in April in order to be ready for the new arrival. Now she didn't have to go to work until September.

Her first second-season show was done again, as in 1967's initial presentation, with Jim Nabors.

Now we'll quote critic Harriet Van Horne on that first show:

"In common with most comedians, Miss Burnett falters when faced with the simple business of introducing guests and bantering with the audience. She brought on Jim Nabors . . . with so fulsome a tribute to his heart, mind, and noble spirit that you half expected to see a rich white light pouring out of him."

The second season of the *Carol Burnett Show* was every bit as successful as the first. The midway point of the series came at year's end, with every expectation that CBS would not only announce intentions of having it go into its third season, but would yield to Carol's insistence for an earlier time slot. Carol's argument was:

"I like a kid audience. Sure, I don't mind a little blue material but I'm not interested in getting risqué on the air. I'm really a very square person. I've never smoked pot or seen a stag film. I've never even seen *Hair*. I'm really out of it."

What Carol was driving at was that the younger generation wasn't going to be corrupted by listening to the occasional double entendre, which was part of the reason why the show was such a hit. After all, CBS was fortified with a battery of censors armed with blue pencils to chop objectionable material from scripts. Then, too, there were the film editors who backed up the censors after taping was completed. The censors couldn't prevent what happened during the spontaneous question-and-answer periods at the start of the shows, but they saw to it that anything not in good taste was chopped.

Yet sometimes in their eagerness to keep the show clean the censors made things worse. For example, in a scene that Carol and Harvey Korman played, Carol was a nudist standing behind a board and Korman, a reporter, was interviewing her.

KORMAN: What do you do for amusement?

CAROL: We have Saturday night dances.

KORMAN: How do you nudists dance?

CAROL: Ver-ry carefully.

The censors didn't like that. Carol's writers wanted to know if the boys with the blue pencils had any suggestions. One of them said, "I have a line that will clean it up." The line—as it was actually telecast—was:

"Cheek to cheek."

While Carol was rehearsing one evening at the studio just before the Christmas-New Year's break, Jim Nabors dropped over at dinnertime. Jim, Carol, Joe, and a few other people went to a nearby restaurant, then returned to the set. They went back by way of the scene dock, the loading platform for props used on different CBS shows. There was a huge gift-wrapped package at least ten feet long, five feet wide, and six feet high. They all stopped to look at it. Carol assumed that since the Smothers Brothers were taping that night, the package was a prop for their show. The package had a big ribbon tied around it and an enormous card.

Nabors said, "Let's look at the card."

Carol read the message. It said: CAROL AND JOE

"Dumb me," Carol says, "I thought, 'Isn't that funny!' But it never occurred to me it was *Joe and me*! Jim casually suggested, 'Why don't you open it?' And I protested, 'Why, we can't touch that!' Then I looked at him and at it, and I realized it *was* for Joe and me. 'It must be a gag,' I thought. 'There are probably some people inside.'

"Then we opened it and, would you believe a 1929 Model A Ford car! A real, honest-to-goodness *working* car! A year before, I had said how much I love those cars and one of these days I'm gonna get me one. And Joe said the same thing. Neither of us thinking—not dreaming—that Jim would *ever* . . . It took Jim a year, but he got it for us for Christmas. And he knew my favorite color is green and he had it painted green."

Carol and Joe named the car *Mavis*, after his mother, who passed away in June 1968 at the age of seventy-three. In the time since they got the surprise Yule gift from Jim Nabors, Carol and Joe have driven the car to the most elegant places—at times when they were dressed in ultraformal clothes and with Joe's two sons sitting in the rumble seat.

"There we come in *Mavis*, chug-chug, clunk-clunk-clunk," Carol said. "We love it. We absolutely adore the car. When Joe drives and it backfires, the kids all yell, 'Daddy's home!' It really sounds like St. Valentine's Day in Chicago. The poor parking boys at Chasen's and the Bistro can't start it. They don't know how it works. And we go pluh, pluh, pluh past the Jet Set and the Rollses. It's kind of reverse snobbism, like me going into Bonwit Teller's in levis."

As the *Carol Burnett Show* barreled into the last of its hourly segments for the 1968–'69 season, Carol received a letter datelined Cambridge, Massachusetts. It was from Harvard University's Hasty Pudding Club and they wanted Carol to know that she had been selected as their nineteenth annual Woman of the Year.

Carol flew to Boston on February 23 and accepted the distinguished award. Then, after she finished the last of her shows, Carol looked forward to a long vacation from work.

That year was going to be more fun than any past summer, for Joe had finally bought what he'd been promising his wife—an oceanfront home in Malibu Beach. The house, with a spacious sundeck, had just one fault so far as Carol was concerned. That was the interior décor—just too much purple. But that was the way they bought the place from the former owner—with purple brocade chairs in the living room (contrasting sharply against the garish silver tones of the sofa) and a master bedroom with purple velvet drapes and bedspread.

Carol shivered at the sight of all that purple—in a

beach house, no less. But by then she'd had enough experience as a decorator to know what had to be done. She'd just finished refurnishing the house in Beverly Hills so that it no longer was Betty and Harry's house but Carol and Joe's. All Carol needed was time to make the Malibu Beach digs conform to the Hamiltons' tastes.

One of the selling points when Carol and Joe inspected the house before buying it was its Olympic-size pool—something they felt was far safer for their small children than the beach and the crashing Pacific breakers. It was in that pool that Carrie was taught to swim by Joe's sons, and in time to come the boys taught their stepsisters Jody Ann and Erin Kate, in their turn, to swim.

But that summer of 1969 wasn't all fun and play for Carol. Along about the middle of July she found that she could no longer lope along the beach with the children or spring over the sandy turf behind the house to launch a kite for the kids.

Pain—excrutiating pain—had slowed Carol down to a hobble. The doctor told her that she had Morton's Toe— a neurological condition of the foot caused by pressure on a nerve. Corrective surgery was performed—and once again Carol Burnett was walking around on crutches.

"I know Morton's Toe sounds terribly unglamorous," Carol said. "But it's not uncommon. Athletes get it. But it's *not* athlete's foot!"

At least when the foot healed Carol was able to wear a closed shoe—and just in time to start rehearsals and taping for her third year of the *Carol Burnett Show*.

There were no problems with the show in its third year either, although on a few occasions the ratings didn't reach their accustomed peaks. But Carol wasn't worried. The show was still ahead of the competition and she was perceptive enough to know of the hill-and-valley movements of even the most popular TV shows.

Thus Carol's show went into its fourth year. But not before she had a slight blowout with CBS about censorship. Yet that had nothing to do with her show but, rather, a taping she had made in December for Merv

Griffin's talk show that was aired Christmas night. Carol had appeared in the interests of a campaign called People For Peace, which was voicing pleas against violence and calling on the public to send such messages to Mrs. Martin Luther King, who, in turn, would deliver them to then-President Richard M. Nixon at the White House.

Well, Carol went on Griffin's show wearing a People for Peace armband which was too big for her arm and kept falling down. So she ended up holding it. Then she made her appeal—a fifteen-second urging to send those messages to Mrs. King. Carol's whole Christmas was spoiled when she tuned in Griffin's show and watched her lips flipping like in the good old silent-picture days.

"I felt like an absolute jerk," Carol said. "It made me look like I said something dirty, or off-color—or maybe un-American."

Well, if Carol's Christmas was spoiled, that was no reason why Robert D. Wood's Yule shouldn't be scrooged. Fuming, Carol dialed all the way to Wood's home in Connecticut and unlimbered a broadside that made the Christmas tree shake in the living room. Wood only happened to be CBS-TV network president and he wasn't accustomed to being reamed out by the hired hands—not even those on the payroll for a hundred thou.

Believe it or not, Wood claimed that he was just as stunned about the whole thing as Carol was. He promised to get to the bottom of it—and soon did. It turned out that the culprit was William Tankersley, head of the CBS program-practices department. He had deleted Carol's appeal because "long established network policy prohibits appeals for active support of any cause without prior consultation with the network."

Merv Griffin was incensed too. He said:

"The President can ask for mail but Carol Burnett cannot. . . ."

In the end, CBS sent Carol an apology. But that didn't change the fact that she had a lousy Christmas. Yet as the New Year, 1970, came in, Carol could look ahead once more to a very good year, which it was destined to be.

By now Carol—with much credit to her great writers—was beginning to create a gallery of really terrific characters. They were vibrant, animated persons who moved about the stage hilariously recast in the buffooning image of Carol Burnett. No one was beyond imitation, especially the classic Hollywood heartburners.

Some of her most memorable victims up to then and in the time since have been such film imortals as Joan Crawford, being spoofed by Carol in a comedic melodrama titled "Mildred Fierce"; Barbara Stanwyck in "Double Calamity"; Rita Hayworth in "Golda," and by no means last, Gloria Swanson in "Sunset Boulevard." As Nora Desmond (for Miss Swanson's role in the film), Carol has had the most fun acting out the neuroses of a faded but unbowed movie queen tottering around her museumlike mansion with the mirage of autograph-seekers leaping out of every cobwebbed corner. And, of course, her faithful manservant, Eric Von . . . no, that's really Harvey Korman, Miss Burnett's talented coconspirator.

"Harvey and I are as married as two performers can be," Carol said with genuine admiration for her sidekick. "He's to me what Carol Reiner, Howard Morris, and Imogene Coca were to Sid Caesar. Harvey can play anything."

Yet so can Carol. Those make-believe experiences that she had as a kid when she spent so many afternoons at the movies and then went home to act out the parts have come in handy in her letter-perfect parodies of those old movie stars and their films.

"Now, on the show, I can really do them right," Carol said. "All I have to say is, 'I'd like to be Betty Grable,' and we do our version of *The Dolly Sisters*, which is really any 20th Century-Fox musical, since they were all the same story. So it's really an extension of my childhood, which is a great way to grow up."

Carol has never taken bows for the skits without making certain her talented writers are given credit.

"The writers are very important," Carol stressed. "Being a writer for a variety show is the hardest job in the world because practically everything's written from scratch. That's why we don't have the same writers all the time. After a while they get sapped and need a change—maybe like going over to Flip Wilson."

Joe Hamilton estimates he has had about forty writers for the show since the beginning. And he plans to continue shifting them "to keep our material fresh and funny." Or, as Carol put it:

"Dramatic actors think it's easy to jump in and be funny about anything. I think it's at least as difficult as doing drama. Most people cry at the same thing, but no two people laugh at the same thing. I'm a good listener, though, so if something grates, I'll hear it. Sometimes we'll just write on our feet as we work on a sketch, making lots of changes. Other times, we just add the whipped cream to what the writers have come up with, like the take-off we did on *Love Story*, which is one of my all-time favorites."

Since Carol Burnett was a little girl, one of her all-time favorite actresses was Rita Hayworth. And when Carol did her spoof of the sultry screen siren in her hit movie *Gilda*, what followed was a replay, of sorts—but in reverse —of the fan letter Miss Burnett had sent to an unbelieving Jim Nabors before they knew each other. Carol almost flipped out when the telegram arrived.

"I loved it," the wire read. "It was hilarious. Congratulations."

It was signed Rita Hayworth. And that opened negotiations with Miss Hayworth for an appearance on Carol's show that following February, which was a tremendous feather in the Burnett bonnet, since Rita had faced the TV cameras only once before—for an interview with Sandor Vanocur in the early days of *First Tuesday*.

Miss Hayworth's presence on the program—in dowdy charwoman's apparel—was merely one of many notable achievements for Carol Burnett in 1971. But before we leave 1970, let's take a look at one of Carol's September shows. She was doing a smiling, frozen-faced characterization of a First Lady. Not that this was Miss Burnett's first spoof of a President's wife. Lady Bird Johnson had previously been the butt of Burnett's buffoonery—and Mrs. Johnson was said to have been just as furious as Pat Nixon over Carol's imitation. But not for the same reason.

Mrs. Johnson's fury was actually directed at her husband, because Lyndon had not had the foresight to install videotaping equipment in the White House so that Carol's apery of Lady Bird could have been preserved for the National Archives and, above all, the Johnson Library at the University of Texas in Austin and the LBJ Ranch on the banks of the Perdinales.

Mrs. Nixon was angered because her husband *had* had the equipment installed, and had given orders to the Signal Corps to videotape every single telecast that made any reference to the First Family. Nixon engaged in that taping activity so that he and his family could be placed in a TV collection for the National Archives, as well as for the Presidential library he hoped would be built for him after he left office.

15

The CBS television network had promised Carol Burnett an earlier time slot, but there it was 1971—the fourth year of her show had reached its season finale—and she still was on 10 to 11 P.M. every Monday night.

Finally, however, the network decided to deliver on its promise, provided that changes were made in Carol's format to appeal to a "younger" audience. But Joe Hamilton put CBS on notice that he had no intention of turning his wife's show into *Howdy Doody*. Carol herself said she wouldn't compromise the superb sketch comedy routines and their adult flavor for the sake of accommodating a larger audience of teenyboppers.

However, by this time Carol had reached a conclusion which threatened to alter at least one aspect of the show:

"It isn't a question anymore of getting big-name guests on a TV show. It's doubtful whether the guest stars do much for the ratings, unless its Richard Burton and Elizabeth Taylor. It's basically a question of who's going to work well with the show. Some of the big names are impossible to work with and we really don't try for the impossibly big names. We have the writers, who make the show in the first place."

But Carol does more than her bit to "make the show" what it really is. Or, as said by *The New York Times'* Robert Berkvist:

"The Burnett talent . . . frequently transforms a lowly bit of funny business into high comedy. Miss Burnett's trim frame is home to a keen sense of the absurd, a genius for exaggeration, impeccable timing, and a wondrously plastic face that can sneer, simper, slobber, and sulk with equal facility—a face that has launched a thousand *shticks*."

Well, the big news of 1971 was the reunion of Carol Burnett and Julie Andrews for another delightful TV fling, their first since their Carnegie Hall appearance in 1962; nearly a whole decade had passed.

CBS turned the trick by getting New York's spanking new Philharmonic Hall at Lincoln Center for the show. The network had first tried to stage the first ladies of song and comedy in London's Palladium but couldn't work an opening into its heavy schedule.

Although the show was slotted for airing in late fall, Carol and Julie had to do their thing on July 1 because that was Philharmonic Hall's only available time for electronic-medium capers.

I was at Philharmonic that Thursday for the long hours of rehearsal and the taping. It was a wondrous sight to see Miss Burnett and Miss Andrews toiling together, dancing with such vigor that they were actually panting for air when they were finished with the routines. Carol was a scream with her spoof of an octogenarian named Madame Abernell, a famed modern dancer, giving her eightieth or ninetieth farewell performance in a skit called "Electra and the Passions Of the Gods." Many observers suspected that she was doing a Martha Graham takeoff.

Another comic episode had Carol as a cellist and Julie a violinist in an orchestra. Carol was complaining about splinters in her body stocking, while her husband, the percussionist, was having an affair with Julie. But most of all I enjoyed the nonsensical exchanges of Carol and Julie:

JULIE: Tell me, dear, what have you been doing

192

with yourself all these years? Are you still in the entertainment business?

CAROL: I'm in television.

JULIE: Oh, what a shame! I've been in motion pictures.

CAROL: Oh, how nice. Talking?

JULIE: I did *Sound Of Music*.

CAROL: Oh, did that thing ever come off?

During breaks in rehearsal, Carol consented to hold question-and-answer sessions with the audience, a la her own show's style—but not for airing. It was Carol Burnett displaying a sincerity that she has never lacked in her relations with audiences. Carol loves to talk with her fans —on camera or off. As she puts it:

"I love 'em all. They're my lifeblood."

While the question-and-answer periods that start off her shows are designed as a warmup, the home viewer has never seen some of the rollicking stuff that is all too often too hot to leave on the final tape for airing. Carol talks about that:

"For instance, there was a woman who walked on stage to invite me to a love-in. I asked, 'What's a love-in?' And she told me.

"Another woman, who looked like Anna Magnani in drag—she weighed about three hundred and fifty pounds and wore a high pompadour—wanted to meet Lyle Waggoner. When she saw him, she chased him all up and down the aisles until she caught him, grabbed him, and kissed him.

"Another time, a man stepped up to the stage to sing. He pointed his finger at Harry Zimmerman, our musical director, and said, 'Hit it!' Then he let out with 'Rock-A-Bye Your Baby To A Dixie Melody' and almost rocked the rafters.

"But one of the wildest things that happened was when I innocently let a man in the audience take over. For fifteen minutes no one could stop him. He was flying at

193

least three feet off stage, doing dramatic improvisations while the director was waving a white handkerchief signaling me to 'get him off, get him off.' "

When the *Carol Burnett Show* returned to the air in September and launched its fifth season, CBS not only set it back from 10 P.M. to 8 P.M., but also changed its day—from Monday to Wednesday.

But that did nothing for Carol's ratings—except hurt them. Wednesday turned out to be the lousiest night of the week for Burnett fans, and what was even more annoying was that early evening hour. Housewives were still washing the dinner dishes and the kids were still doing their homework.

Alarmed at the audience dropoff, CBS made a mid-season switch sooner than any of the people on the show expected. As of December 16, the *Carol Burnett Show* was playing a 10-to-11 P.M. Saturday night schedule, which made everyone happy—most especially CBS. For now the network was beginning to shape a Saturday night presentation of comedy that in time *Newsweek* was to call a "murderers' row" of comic shows. With fun time starting off with *All In The Family,* followed by *M*A*S*H,* then the *Mary Tyler Moore Show,* the *Bob Newhart Show,* and finally the *Carol Burnett Show,* CBS indeed had scored an unprecedented coup with comedy. Or, as *Newsweek* put it:

"America hasn't had so much fun since Uncle Miltie used to drop in on those long-ago Tuesday nights. These days, restaurant and theater owners are blaming their Saturday-night attendance slippage on the fuel shortage. Nielsen knows better: the ratings reveal that some fifty million stay-at-homes are hooked on a three-hour fix of laughing gas. From Carroll O'Connor to Carol Burnett, CBS has marshaled a murders' row of TV comedy that has made Saturday the happiest night of the week."

CBS didn't have to be choosy when it put *Julie and Carol at Lincoln Center* on the air. It picked December 7, a Monday night, at 8:30. Critics raved about the show, using such laudatory language as "pure entertainment," "an unusually pleasant hour," "very effective comedy," "slick," "well-paced," and "wondrously pleasing."

Carol could look back on 1971 and say it was another wonderful year. She had even fulfilled that mania to be on the legitimate stage again. Nothing like her outings in *Once Upon A Mattress* or *Fade Out-Fade In*, because Carol had had her fill of long-running Broadway theater. Her roots were in California now, so except for occasional appearance at the Dallas State Fair, Carol's only stage work was limited to the Huntington Hartford Theater in Los Angeles.

Her success that summer in a brief run of *Plaza Suite*, in which she costarred with George Kennedy, temporarily quenched her thirst for stage work. Moreover, it didn't drain her strength and energy as theater work in the East had done when Carol was doubling in the weekly TV grind at the same time. She could still dash home to Beverly Hills—or Malibu Beach—and be with the children. Or entertain sister Chris, who by this time had gone through a traumatic experience since her days at Moravian. Chris, you see, was never keen about college.

"Chris always talked about wanting to get married," Carol revealed. "I had to force her to go to college. I told her that there was plenty of time to find a man and settle down."

But Moravian didn't do for Chris what Carol had hoped it would.

Chris said she simply loved going to *that* college—but the reason wasn't educational.

"I must say, for a girl" (who liked boys as much as Chris did) "it's the only place to go. It's coed. Right across the river in Lehigh, an all-men university, and twenty minutes away is Lafayette College—all men. I was only there two years. My grades weren't good. I was just living it up. Then I decided to go to a New York secretarial school. I started, but then I met Hutch. . . ."

Chris was speaking about Will Hutchins, star of the

TV potboiler *Sugarfoot* and of *Hey, Landlord!* At the time Chris met Hutchins, he was playing in *Never Too Late* on Broadway. And then they were married, but not for long. Yet long enough for Chris to have a baby.

"Our little courtship and marriage," explained Chris, "ruined my secretarial career, which I wasn't too hip on anyway."

So Chris brought little Jennifer to Los Angeles, "Just five minutes away from Sissy." Since then, Chris has been a regular visitor at the Hamiltons. And Jennifer enjoys playing with Carrie Louise, Jody Ann, and Erin Kate.

Chris said she will forever be grateful to Carol for "loving me with patience and understanding." Carol hadn't mentioned all of the details surrounding that episode in 1958 when she "kidnaped" Chris from their mother and brought her to New York. Chris provides us with those missing details and some fresh insights into a young woman's most poignant memory of her childhood.

It began with that day in New York when Chris learned from Carol that there was no going back to her mother in California.

"It was New Year's Eve day," Chris recalled. "Sissy and I were walking back to the apartment from the grocer's carrying huge bags. I said, 'Sissy, I do have to go back to school, you know. Isn't it about time we talked about my going back?'

"Sissy said, 'I have something to tell you.' I knew right then what was coming. The tears started falling. I didn't want to face it. I raised cain. I made terrible scenes. Sissy promised me braces for my teeth and the whole bit. I thought that was jolly, but I still wanted to go home.

"Even though we didn't have much and I'd have more in New York, I still loved my mother and I missed her and I wanted to go back. I was horrible to Sissy and she was very good and very kind. I remember saying something terrible to her, and my brother-in-law, Don, came across the room and slapped my face.

"I'd never been hit like that, but I knew I deserved it. I called Mama, crying and pleading to come home. But she was firm. She said, 'Honey, you just have to stay there. Sissy can do a lot more for you than I can.'" It just tore her up to do that. She had nothing else. I was the only thing she had—and she gave me up. It was the greatest gift any human being can give.

"Finally Sissy gave me an ultimatum—the only one that could have made me stay. She said, 'All right, Chrissie, if you get back on the plane and go home, you'll never see me again.' Well, that did it. I thought, *Dear God, I can't give Sissy up*.

"One night shortly after I had more or less resigned myself, I was asleep on the couch in the living room. I was sound asleep, but about 3:30 A.M. I sat straight up in bed and something said to me, *Your mom is going to die*.

"I got up and went to the little desk in the living room, turned on the light, and wrote her a letter. I said, 'Mama, I love you no matter what I've said or done to you; please don't let it hurt you.' I just wrote everything I wanted to say to her and probably never had.

"She got the letter shortly before she died. I am so grateful I had the chance to tell her. A lot of times you don't get the chance. Mama was a good person. She couldn't afford medical attention . . . all that expensive dope they give you for the pain.

"When she had pain, she drank. She was good, but weak, and she loved us. She died January 10."

Chris said that after Carol sent her to the Episcopalian school in New Jersey, life took a severe and dramatic turn for her.

"Boy, were they ever strict!" Chris said about the school's staff. "I've never seen such discipline! They were tender at first. They knew Mama had just died, so they were a little lenient, but not too much. They knew they had to keep me busy and keep my mind off of it. It was a little too strict, but I took to the religion right away.

"We saw boys only four times a year, which was a real switch for me. Once a month we were allowed to spend a weekend at home. I really learned *appreciation*. That little apartment was pure luxury. Going to the bathroom when I wanted to, watching television, staying up late, and eating real meals."

But Carol Burnett was not all that easy going. What freedom Chris had at home was delegated to her by Carol's *sister* role. But when she was Chris's *mother*, things were different.

"Sissy was very maternal," Chris said. "She was always after me to clean my room, fully convinced I had bodies buried under my clothes. She threatened to have the Sanitation Department take me away.

"The three of us really had a lot of fun. We were full of beans and always putting each other on. We'd dress up like monsters, go out on the fire escape, and wave to the people on Eighth Avenue. Some of our poorest days in New York were the most fun."

"The welfare people sent a worker to check on me. I was asked if I was happy and I answered, 'Yep.' That's when it dawned on me I really *was* happy."

On a more recent day, Chris and Jennifer were over at Carol's. They were talking and while Jennifer and Carrie were playing around the Christmas tree, Carol turned to her sister.

"You know, Chrissie," Carol said, pointing at Carrie, "she will never know what we went through. She's lucky in a way, but in a way it's kind of sad. There are so many things she won't appreciate."

By now Joe's two sons were no longer living with Carol and their father. They have grown up and gone off to college. The house is quiet again, as quiet as it can be with three growing young daughters romping about. Carrie is now going on twelve, Jody will soon be nine, and Erin Kate is nearing her seventh birthday. Carol is trying to raise her little girls just as she raised Chrissie:

"They all go to private school. There's no hassle in the morning about what they'll wear, because they all wear uniforms. Do I wish I had boys? No. I do worry about the children and the future, of course. Things change so fast today. When I think of what I knew at Carrie's age and what she knows, it's scary. And you worry about the drug thing, too, because there's no escape. It's everywhere. You try to instill the right feelings, and then all you can do is hope for the best."

If her fear of the drug problem wasn't enough, Carol was suddenly confronted by a pair of stories published in two fan magazines that claimed she would condone use of marijuana by her children. Carol charged that they falsely represented her views about pot—and she promptly filed twin five-million-dollar suits against the mags.

In general practice such litigations have a way of fading away after the stark announcement that a star is suing a fan book. They usually end up with an apology— and a flow of favorable stories about the entertainer. Which is the way Miss Burnett allowed it to happen in this instance.

Carol, of course, has been the darling of the fan books since even before she joined the *Garry Moore Show*. Some writers haven't always treated her too complimentarily, especially after her romance with Joe Hamilton became a headline story. Now and then fan books will revive the story under such titles as "How Carol and Joe Survived the Ugly Gossip." But it isn't even beneath the so-called slicks to remind readers as much as a dozen years after it happened, as *Newsweek* did recently when it cheered Carol as "our female Chaplin" and raved about her talents, etc. Yet it didn't fail to let it be said:

"Burnett's personal life, however, had become a bit messy. Her marriage to Don Saroyan, a UCLA classmate who had tagged along on her Eastern odyssey, had already ended when she met Joe Hamilton. . . . When Hamilton left his wife and eight children for Carol, the gossip columnists gleefully cast her in the role of home-wrecker. . . ."

Carol takes what criticism comes her way these days with a philosophical stance:

"People still criticize me, I realize that. And I'm sorry they can't see my side, only what's in the paper. But you can't let public opinion run your life. Joe and I just hoped, very hard, that eventually everybody would be happy and, thank God, everybody is."

Jim Nabors remembers one fan-magazine story that had deliberately tried to "make something dirty out of a perfectly wonderful friendship" between him and Carol. He was referring to a cover story titled: THE LOVE THAT CAROL BURNETT AND JIM NABORS CAN NO LONGER HIDE

Nabors said he was furious when he saw the cover. But when he read the story he changed his mind:

"Inside—if you got that far—the article ended up saying that we were like brother and sister. It's so darned hard, out here, to have friends in the first place. I mean, real ones—not just one-sided affairs. Especially in this business, with everybody's tremendous ego. I was terribly bugged that this particular magazine couldn't respect a nice friendship."

But Carol's humor calmed Jim. It happened that Carol had seen the article, too:

"Joe's boys had brought the magazine home and I read the story," Carol said. "I got hysterical laughing. I didn't know if Jim had seen it or not, but I called him and I said very seriously, 'Listen, Joe's on his way over to kill you . . . do you have any last words?'

"He didn't have the faintest idea what I was talking about and he got all shook. Then I couldn't help laughing. I confessed, 'Well, the boys brought home a magazine and on the cover it insinuates that we've got a big hot romance going—so there's nothing else for Joe to do! But I thought I'd call you and warn you. . . .'"

Nabors said that Carol had sounded pretty convincing, except that he had already read the story and seen that it was a puff of nothing. Then, too, he didn't get shook because he heard Joe laughing in the background while Carol was talking.

Perhaps it's a sign of maturity in Carol Burnett to accept annoying stories about her with a smile. Some years ago she felt hurt when critical or biting pieces appeared in magazines or newspapers. She still doesn't like criticism. Who does? But she doesn't let any story disturb her equilibrium.

If a lie, an outright lie such as the marijuana stories, is written, then she'll send her lawyer after the culprit.

And she has that same detached, easygoing philosophy about many other things in life—including the Nielsen ratings, which make or break TV performers.

"I gave up worrying about the ratings years ago," Carol said. "Worrying doesn't help. You just do your best. I don't care what happens, really. What happens—I'm sounding like Doris Day—will happen. We've gone for six years with the series, and if it's supposed to continue on Saturday nights, it will. I frankly didn't think it would last a year."

Though Carol said that just when her show was put into the Saturday night spot, she feels the same way today. But Carol hasn't had to concern herself about bad ratings since that time. Even if she were the worrying kind, she'd have had no concern. For Carol's show has been CBS's most successful presentation from the standpoint of audience acceptability, ratings, and advertiser revenues.

And that became a fact long before the 1971-'72 season ended on the happy note from joyful CBS that the *Carol Burnett Show* was heading into its seventh year on the air in the fall.

Meanwhile, Carol had gotten a phone call from a famous movie star:

"I didn't know him very well, and usually when a movie star calls someone in TV they want you to do a benefit or something," Carol said.

The caller was Walter Matthau.

"Caaarolll? Ya still love me? . . . Good. Wanna do a movie with me?"

"Do I? Is the Pope Catholic?"

The movie was to be *Pete 'N' Tillie*, pitting Carol and

Walter as a couple whose marriage founders on the rocks of the unexpected, a bittersweet tale.

"I read the script," Carol said. "I liked it. And I went ahead and did it. . . ."

16

Tillie Schlaine was an inhibited single girl till her uninhibited friend, Gertrude, fixed up a romance for her with Pete Seltzer, an irrepressible prankster. There are a lot of laughs in the early going, even when the romance turns into marriage, a marriage which lasts for ten years and produces a son, Charlie.

The death of Charlie, at age nine, leads to the breakdown of the marriage, which is followed by an almighty bustup between Gertrude and Tillie—the cause being Gertrude's belief that Tillie has winkled out the secret closest to her friend's heart: Gertrude's true age. And it does not stop at name-calling—the two women wrestle in puddles, sling mud, spray each other with garden hoses, and, biggest insult of all, Tillie pulls off Gertrude's wig.

"They offered us doubles for the fight scene," Carol explained, "but we decided to slug it out in person."

The result was one of the epic slam-bang battles between two broads ever staged in films. Despite her past infirmities—a herniated disc, quadruple leg fracture, and Morton's Toe—Carol Burnett, playing Tillie Schlaine, performed that backbreaking scene with Geraldine Page as though she were approaching twenty, not forty.

Although the people over at Universal Pictures were delighted with Burnett and Matthau as a costarring film couple, Carol was again critical of herself, just as she had been after doing *Who's Been Sleeping In My Bed*? She complained:

"I didn't like me in it and I wish I could do it again. It's tough to fight an image that's been built up over the years. People were expecting me to come on screen swinging from a chandelier and I think I was inhibited by that, to the point of underplaying Tillie by stifling myself. She could have had more personality. But it was a happy experience."

Carol loved working with Walter. The picture opened around the country just before Christmas of 1972 and received high critical acclaim.

The overwhelming opinion of the critics was that Carol Burnett handled her dramatic part exceptionally well and, of course, the knock-down, drag-out fight with Miss Page was certainly a scene that Carol had no trouble with—after all the practice she'd had with her weekly acrobatic TV sketches.

During her career Carol Burnett had very few opportunities until *Pete 'N' Tillie* to sink her teeth into a dramatic role. In that film she demonstrated a remarkable feeling for fine character interpretation—and a promise of a future career that could readily go beyond music and comedy.

Yet even now Carol keeps alive the hope that she may do another Broadway musical. Not with the enthusiasm of old, but the idea and desire are still in her mind. Carol knows that the biggest drawback in making the trek back to the Great White Way is the children. They are settled in school in Beverly Hills, and it would be unfair, she feels, to leave them for the year or so which she would have to be in New York or to uproot them from the Coast and bring them east with her.

Even more realistically from the standpoint of the *Carol Burnett Show*, how could she do the weekly segments—unless CBS agreed to switch production to New York? In that unlikely event, still another problem must be faced: Who foots the bill to move the cast and crew to New York?

204

So it seems very doubtful that Carol Burnett will do anything on Broadway for a long time—except come for a visit now and then. But she has found a way to satisfy the urge for the stage whenever it stirs her juices to perform: She flits over to the Huntington Hartford Theater in Los Angeles, as she did in the summer of '71 when she teamed up with George Kennedy in *Plaza Suite* and again the summer of '73 when she returned to the same stage for a three-week fling with old TV sidekick Rock Hudson in the musical *I Do, I Do.*

Occasionally, too, you'll catch Carol winging across an ocean to such faraway places as Australia, as she did on a fall day of 1973 with the cast and crew of her show. That was a very special thing, for the *Carol Burnett Show* had the distinction of being the first television company from the United States presented in the fabulous Sydney Opera House, which had been dedicated by Queen Elizabeth only a few days before the taping.

By now Carol had an added regular on her show—Tim Conway, who is always at his best doing his shuffling-old-man routine. In Australia Conway scored heavily with the audience of nearly three thousand by impersonating an aging symphony conductor, while Carol and Harvey Korman flourished in slapstick when they took off as the famous acting team of "Funt And Mundane."

Back in 1963 a blind quote appeared in a newspaper feature on Carol Burnett. The interviewer identified her source as "a TV producer," and credited him with saying about Miss Burnett:

"Imagine how far this dame will get by 1973! She will be Ethel Merman and Lucille Ball and Jackie Gleason and Sid Caesar all wrapped up in one. She'll be at the top of the entertainment world. . . ."

Nostradamus couldn't have predicted that future more accurately. Miss Burnett was on top of the entertainment world in 1973—and 1974. And she still is at this very moment.

Carol Burnett certainly has a lot to be thankful for:

her husband, the children they've had together, and her remarkable career as one of our most lovable, most talented female clowns.

What we have in Carol Burnett is an individual unlike anyone who has preceded her in the entertainment world. She is unique because of the innumerable imaginary tenants who inhabit her mind and spring out with endless regularity like old friends—the bespectacled Girl Scout leader; the frumpy charwoman stumbling and bumbling along with her mop and pail; the improbably tempestuous Latin sex kitten Charro togged out in blonde Afro, halter, and hip huggers, who vibrates at the slightest provocation; the thrill-seeking housewife waiting for the weekly obscene phone call; and all the other wonderful characters she has created and enacted.

Then, too, there is her seemingly inexhaustible stock of ghosts from the show world that once was—Crawford, Stanwyck, Grable, Swanson, MacDonald, Hayworth, Temple, and so many others.

But even the biggies of today's show business are not immune to Carol's demolishing spoofery—she has broken up audiences with her imitations of Cher Bono and (God's going to get her for this) even satirized Bea Arthur (Maude), who only happens to work for the same network.

The procession of characters and ideas keep flowing as steadily and powerfully as those waters over Niagara, churning up a tidal wave of fun that makes America seasick with laughter.

How long will this go on?

That's difficult to say. But when you think about reruns, Carol Burnett could be forever.

I'm so glad we had this time together. . . .